KU-711-111

◀ Europe on the move ▶

Exploring Europe

Hereward College
Bramston Crescent
COVENTRY
CV4 9SW

00007865

MANUSCRIPT:

Ciara McLoughlin, Faith Kilford. April 1996.

CARTOONS:

Will (drawings)
Will was born in Anthée, Belgium, on 30 October 1927 and is the author of the adventures of *Tif et Tondu*, which have brought the pages of *Journal de Spirou* to life for the last 50 years. A master from the Golden Age of the Franco-Belgian comic strip, he is also a painter and illustrator. His *Isabel* series, created in 1970, is a masterpiece of poetry and graphic imagination.

Rudi Miel (storyline)
Rudi Miel was born in Tournai, Belgium, on 19 January 1965 and writes the storyline for the adventures of *Charlotte*.

LAYOUT: **Rumeurs.**

Contents

Exploring Europe
An Introduction

Fifteen European countries have joined to form the European Union (EU). Despite differences of culture, customs and experience, they share the desire to live in peace, play a role on the world political stage, improve their living and working conditions and strive for greater justice in the world.

This booklet is intended for the youth of Europe. It is the young who will be called upon to continue its construction: the Union is only what we all decide to make it.

One of Europe's assets is our richness of cultures, traditions, and languages. It is very important that we recognize this and appreciate the other countries of the Union. Evidence of what happens in the absence of understanding and acceptance can be seen in the activities of extremist groups and xenophobia in general.

In preparing this booklet we asked young Europeans to write down the first five things that sprang to mind when they thought about a particular country. Naturally, many of the answers were obvious. While giving factual information about each of the 15 countries this brochure also attempts to address some of these typical answers.

1996 is the centenary of the comic-strip. We therefore asked Will, a renowned comic-strip artist from Belgium, to create a short story about each country as he sees it through his 50 years of creating comic-strips. His drawings are his view, not an official view of the European Commission, and we hope that through this mixture of facts, cliches and humour you will be encouraged to find out for yourself about the countries of the EU. Have a nice trip !

Lastly, the brochure deals briefly with what the Union has achieved — progress that has come far, but which we can build upon.

AH, BELGIUM, LAND OF THE COMIC STRIP! ALL MY CHILDHOOD HEROES CAME FROM HERE – TINTIN, LUCKY LUKE, SPIROU AND FANTASIO.

BRUSSELS

WHY DON'T YOU LOOK WHERE YOU'RE GOING? SOMETHING CATCH YOUR EYE?

NO, IT'S ALL RIGHT...

COMIC STRIP MUSEUM

?

A diamond cutter at work, Antwerp.
Eureka Slide

Belgium's coastline.
Isopress

Belgium

POPULATION
10 million

CAPITAL
Brussels

★

Founding member

The highest mountain in Belgium is the Signal de Botrange (694 m) and the main rivers are the Scheldt and the Meuse.

LAND

The Kingdom of Belgium lies in north-western Europe, bounded to the north by the Netherlands, to the east by Luxembourg and Germany, to the south by France and to the west by the North Sea. Belgium has an area of 30 519 km². Inland from the coast are fertile polders, the sandy Flanders plain, and the heaths and woods of the Campaign. Between these northern lowlands, the wooded Ardennes and Belgian Lorraine in the south, lie the alluvial central plateaux.

PEOPLE

Belgium has a population of 10 million and an average population density of 328 inhabitants per km². Although the population density is among the highest in Europe, it varies from an average 50 inhabitants per km² living in the wooded Ardennes to 10% of the entire population living in the capital city, Brussels. Of the 920 000 foreigners living in Belgium, the majority come from other countries within the Union, 23% of them from Italy.

The official language in Flanders, which is in the northern half of the country, is Dutch. The official language of the Walloons who inhabit the south, is French. In Brussels, French and Dutch have equal status, although there is a majority of French speakers. There is a small German-speaking minority to the east of the province of Liège and Luxembourg. All three languages are official in Belgium. Approximately 57% of the population are Dutch-speaking and 42% speak French.

ECONOMY

Metal processing is highly developed in Belgium and accounts for 30% of industrial employment. The chemical and electronic industries are also significant. Traditional industries such as textiles in Flanders and glass in Wallonia have been rationalized and modernized; Their origins can be traced back to the medieval cloth makers and Venetian glassblowers. One of Belgium's most famous food exports is chocolate. Chocolate exports contribute significantly to the country's trade balance surplus.

CONSTITUTION AND GOVERNMENT

The Kingdom of Belgium is a parliamentary monarchy. It is a federal State consisting of regions and communities. Legislative power at federal level is exercised jointly by the King, the Chamber of Representatives and the Senate. By the constitutional amendments made in 1993 the number of representatives was reduced to 150 and the number of senators to 71 (the senators being either directly elected or designated by the councils of the communities or coopted). Senators and representatives are no longer allowed to combine their office with membership of a regional or community council. Executive power is vested in the King and his ministers. The King has the right to dissolve the federal parliament. Parliament may force the federal government to resign if the Chamber of Representatives passes a vote of no confidence and at the same time nominates a new prime minister for appointment by the King.

The three regions (Brussels, Flanders and Wallonia) and the three communities (Flemish, French and German-speaking) each have a directly elected legislative assembly, known as the council, and an executive. The Flemish region and community have merged to form a single entity with one council and one executive only.

The Ardennes region is popular for both sport and relaxation.
Van Parys Media

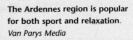

'What are the first five things that spring to mind when you think about Belgium ?'

▶ Brussels - Chocolates - Tintin - Beer - Capital of Europe

Brussels

Many think of Brussels merely in the context of the EU (see below), however, it is also a city filled with interesting museums, markets offering everything from antiques to Middle Eastern spices, and restaurants which some say are among the best in the world. The Grand Place is one of the finest medieval squares in Europe. It was almost completely destroyed in 1695 after Louis XIV's bombardment, but was then rebuilt within 10 years. Many of the old guild houses in the square are now cafes and restaurants, and it was in one of these in 1847 that Marx and Engels wrote *The Communist Manifesto*. Not too far away is the Sablon area, a centre for antique shops and chic cafes. The Atomium is also something people associate with Brussels. This 102 m high construction consisting of nine metal atoms representing the carbon molecule, all linked by staircases, was built in 1958 for the Brussels World Fair. Brussels has a lively nightlife, however many of the best and 'in' places to go are hidden away and known only by word of mouth.

The Grand Place, Brussels.

Van Parys Media

Chocolates

The Spanish conquistador, Hernando Cortes, is widely credited with introducing chocolate to Europe. Historians cannot, however, agree on the creator of the filled chocolates which have made Belgium famous. Many believe it to be the Belgian Jean Neuhaus. Neuhaus began experimenting with different recipes in his family's chemist shop where his grandfather had been prescribing chocolate as medicine. Today Neuhaus is one of Belgium's legendary luxury chocolate producers and the site of the old shop is still used by the company in Brussels. Neuhaus is also credited with the creation of the cardboard box or *ballotin* in which chocolates are usually packed. Chocolate is one of Belgium's main food exports and more than 80% of exports go to countries within the European Union.

The elaborate presentation of Belgian chocolates is one reason for their great renown.

Bernard Boccara

Eureka Slide

Beer

It is estimated that there are over 450 different types of Belgian beer. This is just a rough estimate because in Belgium it is traditional to create a new beer or special brew for important occasions. Christmas beers are a good example of this, and beers are often created for the festivities of a marriage or inauguration. This tradition can be traced back to the 1900s, when more breweries existed in Belgium than there were villages. In fact the local brewer often had the dual role of mayor as well. Blanche, Geuze and Kriek are examples of the different varieties of beer that exist today.

Brewing has many different stages, here the beer is being filtered.

Van Parys Media

Tintin

Belgium is the country with the most cartoonists per km² in the world. The comic is considered an art form and is read by people of all ages and from all social classes. *La bande dessinée* has become a part of Belgium's cultural heritage. A beautiful art nouveau building is home to the comic museum, and comic shops abound in Belgium. Hergé, the creator of the legendary cartoon character, Tintin, is himself internationally renowned. The adventures of the little reporter and his dog have been translated into 45 languages and to date 172 million Tintin albums have been sold.

Hergé, and his most famous creation, Tintin.

Capital of Europe

Brussels is home to offices of the European Commission, Parliament, and Council of Ministers. In addition to the 16 000 people who work for the Commission a huge number of translators, lobbyists, printers, lawyers and consultants live and work in Belgium directly because of it. It has been said that for every two 'European' jobs, one Belgian job results. Some developers estimate the need for 2-3 million square metres of office space. NATO and the Western European Union are also based in Brussels, as are numerous multinational corporations, and the city itself supports more press reporters from around the world than any other city (about 800), including Washington DC.

The Christiansborg Palace,
home of the Danish Parliament
and Supreme Court.
C. Andersen

A traditional farmhouse
on the island of Langeland.
Fotostock

DENMARK

POPULATION
5.2 million

CAPITAL
Copenhagen

★

1973

Denmark is a flat country; the highest point rises to 173 m. The longest river is the Gudenå, (160 km long) which rises in central Jutland and flows into Randers Fjord.

LAND

Denmark has an area of 43 080 km². It consists of the Jutland peninsula, which has a 67-km-long frontier with north Germany at its base and numerous islands. The largest of the islands are Zealand, Funen, Lolland-Falster and Bornholm. The country lies between the North Sea, to the west and the Baltic Sea to the east. Altogether it has 7 000 km of coastline. Two autonomous regions belong to the Kingdom of Denmark — Greenland and the Faeroe Islands; they are, however, not part of the European Union.

PEOPLE

Denmark has a population of 5.2 million, excluding Greenland and the Faeroes, and the average population density is 120 people per km². Seventy per cent of the population live in urban areas. One million live in the capital, Copenhagen. There is a German-speaking minority in South Jutland, whose representatives secure about 5% of the vote at local elections in that area. Of the 189 000 foreigners in Denmark, 20% come from Member States of the European Union, predominantly the United Kingdom and Germany. Asians form the largest foreign community however (45 000), followed by Turks (34 000).

The official language is Danish, an unusual characteristic of which is the *stød*, a glottal stop at the end of words.

ECONOMY

Denmark's reputation for being among the world's primary agricultural countries is still valid. However, over the last few decades, industrial exports have exceeded agricultural ones. Danish industry is characteristically composed of small and medium-sized companies. North Sea oil and natural gas are becoming increasingly important to the economy.

CONSTITUTION AND GOVERNMENT

The Kingdom of Denmark is a constitutional monarchy and parliamentary democracy. Legislative power lies jointly with the sovereign (the Queen) and the single-chamber parliament (the Folketing). The 179 members of the Folketing are directly elected by a system of proportional representation for a term of four years. The Queen appoints the prime minister after consultation with party leaders; the prime minister may call fresh elections if the government loses its majority in the Folketing. The Queen also appoints the ministers; each of them is responsible to the Folketing individually, and can be removed from office by a vote of no confidence. The Council of State (the Queen and the ministers) considers all bills and important government measures. Bills passed by the Folketing must be put to a referendum if one third of the members of the Folketing so request. Any citizen may lodge a complaint with the Folketing's ombudsman against arbitrary administrative measures.

Denmark is divided into 14 counties plus the metropolitan region of Copenhagen with Frederiksberg. The Faeroes and Greenland are autonomous regions within the Kingdom of Denmark. They have their own parliaments and, unlike Denmark proper, are not part of the European Union. Greenland has belonged to Denmark since 1721; it obtained home rule following a referendum in 1979.

Kartoffelrækkerne housing from around the turn of the century.
C. Andersen

'What are the first five things that spring to mind when you think about Denmark?'

▶ Vikings - Copenhagen - Hans Christian Andersen - Lego - Football

Eureka Slide

Vikings

Much of today's image of the Viking is mythical. For a start there is no evidence that their helmets were ever decorated with horns as is popularly portrayed. Further, Vikings came from Norway, Sweden and Denmark and yet most people believe the Vikings to have been mainly Danish. There are, however, reasons for this. Ole Worm, a Danish scholar, was a key figure in the diffusion of northern literature concerning the Viking age throughout Europe in the 17th century. He corresponded with historians from many other countries. Before the middle of the 10th century when Harold Bluetooth became the first Danish king to accept Christianity, the Vikings were truly hated and feared throughout Europe. It was as if their paganism was their worst sin. In 1016, Knut the Great, King of Denmark conquered England. Condemnation of the Vikings began to subside as they began to settle and achieved respectability by becoming Christian.

A superbly preserved example of a Viking longboat.

Copenhagen

Denmark's capital is located on the islands of Zealand and Amager and the country is governed from the island of Slotsholmen in the middle of Copenhagen. The Christiansborg Palace has housed the Danish Parliament and Supreme Court since 1928. The surrounding buildings are occupied by government offices and access to the island is by way of bridges across the canals. Danes believe Copenhagen to be the café capital of Europe, however, its beer rather than coffee is the main attraction. Local brews include Carlsberg and Tuborg. The Ny Carlsberg Glyptotek, behind the Tivoli Gardens is a building which is a work of art in itself, quite apart from its vast collection of Impressionist paintings and classical sculpture. Copenhagen has always been a centre of trade and shipping and one of the city's most famous inhabitants keeps an eye on the ships — the statue of the Little Mermaid at Langelinie.

The Tivoli Gardens.

Fotosto

Isopress

Hans Christian Andersen

All over the world people know the stories of the ugly duckling, the princess and the pea and the little mermaid. Andersen's fairy-tales and stories have been translated into more than 100 languages. Born into a poor family in Odense in 1805, he travelled to Copenhagen at the age of 14 with dreams of becoming an actor or ballet dancer. His dreams never came to fruition and some years later he began to write. The manuscript that was to mark his first step on the road to fame, *Fairy-tales for children,* was published in Copenhagen when he was 30 years old. Andersen wrote 24 fairy-tale booklets in his lifetime, the last, just three years before his death in 1875.

Hans Christian Andersen.

Isopress

Lego

There are few people who have not played with plastic Lego bricks at some time in their childhood. The firm that makes Lego actually started as a joiners workshop in West Jutland in the 1930s and most of the Lego company is still owned by the family that founded it. Legoland, situated in the town of Billund has come to be one of Denmark's most famous attractions. A theme park containing both rides and models, it is made entirely from pieces of Lego. Some of the most impressive models include an airport, a Rhineland scene and the faces of the American presidents staring down from Mount Rushmore.

Legoland has particular appeal for the young.

C. Andersen

Football

Denmark has been called a nation of football fans. Soccer is both a popular spectator and participant sport. At the weekends people sit in front of television sets and pore over newspapers to discover the fortunes of their favourite teams in the national leagues and of course the progress of the Danish national team in international games. There are some 300 000 registered football players in Denmark. Before leaving to play in the World Cup in Mexico, the Danish team received an audience with the Queen of Denmark, the Prince Consort and their two sons, both soccer fans. Denmark is a big supplier of players to clubs in Italy, Germany, England and Belgium.

The Rhine Valley at Kaub.
Fotostock

Old and new united, the blue Trabant car
is a poignant symbol of the old East Germany.
Eureka Slide

GERMANY

POPULATION
81.2 million

CAPITAL
Berlin

★

Founding member

*Germany covers an area
of 357 000 km², made up
of mountain areas,
uplands and plains. To
the north the country is
bounded by the North
Sea and the Baltic, to the
south by the Alps, Lake
Constance and the Rhine,
which also forms the
border in the south-west.
The main rivers are the
Rhine, the Danube, the
Elbe, the Weser and the
Moselle. The highest
mountain is the Zugspitze
(2 963 m) in the Alps*

LAND

The Federal Republic of Germany is situated in
the heart of Europe. It has nine neighbours:
Denmark in the north, the Netherlands, Belgium,
Luxembourg and France in the west, Switzerland
and Austria in the south and the Czech Republic
as well as Poland in the east. This central position
has been more pronounced since Germany was
united in 1990.

PEOPLE

Germany has a population of over 80 million,
and is one of the most densely populated
countries in Europe — 225 people per km². The
population is distributed very unevenly; Greater
Berlin, which has been growing rapidly since
Germany's unification and now has 3.4 million
inhabitants, will probably have 8 million by the
end of the millennium.

There are 6.9 million foreigners living in
Germany. The Turks, who number 1.85 million,
have long been the largest foreign community,
followed by people from the States belonging to
the former Yugoslavia, whose number can only
be roughly assessed at one million because of the
many war refugees. Next are the Italians, the
Greeks, Poles, Austrians, Romanians and
Spaniards. Germany owes a great deal to her
foreign workers and businessmen. They have
contributed largely to the country's economic
growth and every year add some DM 100 billion
to the country's gross national product.

German is the official language and there are
many dialects. These can be so different that if a
Frisian or Mecklenburger and a Bavarian were to
speak to one another in pure dialect, they would
have great difficulty understanding each other.

ECONOMY

Germany is experiencing a period of adjustment
at the present time so that the enormous
economic differences between the eastern and
western parts of Germany, in particular the
disparity in levels of salaries and standards of
living, can be eradicated. Germany has a social
market economy. Car production is one of the
major industries as are mechanical engineering,
electrical engineering, and the chemical and
pharmaceutical industries. The iron and steel
industry also has a large part to play in the
economy.

CONSTITUTION AND GOVERNMENT

Germany is made up of 16 *Länder* (States). Each
Land has its own constitution, legislature and
government. The country has a parliamentary
regime, with a bicameral legislature. The Upper
House is the Bundesrat and has 68 seats.
Depending on the population, each *Land* has
between three and six seats. The term of office is
dependent on the individual *Lands'* election
dates. The main legislative body is the Lower
House known as the Bundestag (Federal
Assembly). It has 672 deputies who are elected
for four years by universal adult suffrage using a
system of proportional representation and direct
voting.

Executive authority rests with the federal
government, led by the federal chancellor, who is
elected by an absolute majority of the
Bundestag. He then appoints the other
ministers; The federal President is elected by the
Bundesversammlung (a federal convention)
which meets purely for this purpose and consists
of the Bundestag and an equal number of
members elected by *Land* parliaments. The
president is a constitutional head of State and
has little influence on government.

Each *Land* has its own legislative assembly, with
the right to enact laws except on matters such as
defence, foreign affairs and finance which are the
exclusive right of the federal government.

A car
assembly
line.
Fotostock

'What are the first five things that spring to mind when you think about Germany ?'

▶ Beer - Berlin - Goethe - Motorways - Serious

Van Parys Media

Beer

Lager beers are of German origin and actually take their name from the German *lagern* (to store). The Germans have always prided themselves on the purity of their beer and a ban on chemical additives (*Reinheitsgebot*) has been in operation since 1516. Under single market rules, however, beer from other countries can be sold, whether it is brewed respecting the *Reinheitsgebot* or not. Every year between the last week of September and the first week of October, the city of Munich receives a huge influx of people who have come precisely for the beer and the accompanying party atmosphere. *Oktoberfest*, is the annual beer festival and the occasion attracts large numbers of Germans from the different *Länder*, and tourists from further afield. The beer often comes in huge 1 litre tankards and is served in special tents constructed for the duration. The beer festival is also a good opportunity to see the traditional Bavarian costumes — lederhosen for the men and a dirndl for the women.

Munich's *Oktoberfest*.

Berlin

Under the Yalta agreement, Germany was partitioned into four sectors of Allied control. Although located in the Soviet-controlled area of Germany, Berlin was also divided into four. Two years after the Berlin blockade where the Soviets tried unsuccessfully to starve the Allies into leaving the city, Germany split into the German Democratic Republic (East Germany) and the Federal Republic of Germany (West Germany). West Germany, which was the area the Allies had controlled, moved the capital to Bonn, while (east) Berlin de facto remained the capital of Soviet-controlled East Germany. In the 1950s, 2.5 million people left the East for better wages and a higher living standard, which prompted the laying of foundations for the infamous wall in 1961. By 1980 the barrier included a network of three-metre-high walls and electrified fences extending 45 km through Berlin, 120 km around West Berlin as well as along the whole border with West Germany. When the border between Hungary and Austria came down, East Germans began leaving at a rate of 200 people a night until in November 1989, amid great celebrations, the wall came down for good. Berlin stands as Germany's cultural capital — with over 150 museums, 300 private galleries, an historic film industry and a decadent nightlife scene.

Berlin's 'Love Parade' a techno festival, takes place along its most famous shopping street, the Kurfürstendamm.

The famous Reichstag (with the Brandenburg gate behind) was the focus of one of artist Christo's well known 'wrapping' projects in 1995.

Isopress

Van Parys Media

Motorways

The German autobahn network was the first completely modern highway system consisting of dual roadways separated by a large median area. The idea of the motorway was conceived in Germany in 1926 and incorporated into the plans for the road joining Cologne and Bonn started in 1929. The motorway was opened to traffic in 1932. The 'Reich motor roads' was an integrated highway network of approximately 4 000 kilometres. The original military purpose of the roads can be seen quite clearly in the design — accommodating large traffic volumes and speeds over 165 km per hour, they also bypassed cities and provided limited access. Today, Germany's autobahns enable drivers to cross the country with speed and relative ease.

Goethe

Johann Wolfgang von Goethe was the greatest figure of the German romantic period. He and Friedrich Schiller were the main exponents of the literary movement known as *Sturm und Drang* (storm and stress) which celebrated nature, the sensual self, innovation and rebellion against authority. Goethe was born in Frankfurt am Main in 1749 and spent most of his life in Weimar. His most famous works include *Die Leiden des jungen Werther* (1774), *Iphigenie auf Tauris* (1787), *Wilhelm Meisters Wanderjahre* (1821-29) (Wilhelm Meister's travels) and his greatest drama, *Faust*, the second part of which was completed the year he died, 1832.

Goethe and Schiller.

Isopress

Serious

Almost all countries have a so-called national characteristic which other nationalities like to make fun of. Surprisingly, among the answers to the questionnaire the Germans were the only ones to have theirs mentioned — 'serious' and 'without a sense of humour'. Of course it is impossible to generalize about a whole nation of people. Just as there exists a diversity of language and customs within Germany, there also exists a variety and diversity of people. And the Germans are able to laugh at themselves — a well-known German car manufacturer ran a television advertisement some years ago where a German comedian is telling jokes in a club and no one is laughing; the punchline of the ad is 'We'll stick to what we're good at' i.e making cars. Carnival, celebrated in a number of the German *Länder* is also an opportunity to see the Germans dispelling this myth. At the high-point of Carnival which starts the last Thursday before the beginning of Lent and lasts until Ash Wednesday, it is not unusual to see business people, mothers and their babies, schoolchildren and even the police dressed up in costume and enjoying the festivities. Thursday is the day on which women take control, occupying the town halls and cutting men's ties.

GREECE

The tranquillity of the Acropolis, surrounded by the bustle of modern Athens.
Van Parys Media

POPULATION
10.2 million

CAPITAL
Athens

★

1981

Greece is the only country in the Union which does not share a border with another Member State. Its northern frontier, which is 1 180 km long separates the country from Turkey, Bulgaria, FYROM (the Former Yugoslav Republic of Macedonia) and Albania.

LAND

Greece forms a peninsula in southern Europe, covering an area of 131 990 km². Much of the country is mountainous, and the landscape offers sharp contrasts between the rugged peaks — of which the highest is Mount Olympus (2 917 m) — and the blue waters of the Mediterranean. 44% of the land is used for agriculture and 22% is wooded. The major rivers are the Akheloos and the Aliakmon. To the south, east and west of the mainland lie numerous Greek islands. The largest is Crete, stretching 266 km from east to west.

PEOPLE

Greece has a population of 10.2 million and an average population density of 78 inhabitants per km². It is estimated that almost 40% of the present population of Greece is living outside the country. The main emigration destinations in the past have been the USA, Australia and Germany. The annual population growth rate is rather low.

The official language is modern Greek.

ECONOMY

Agriculture still plays a key role in the Greek economy, as does merchant shipping (1 200 vessels or 5% of the world fleet in 1990). Up to the end of the 1960s, the manufacturing industry consisted largely of family businesses, but since then, Greek industry has made enormous strides and industrial products today account for an ever increasing share of the country's exports. Greece is famous for many of its agricultural products: wine, olives and olive oil, feta cheese, tobacco, walnuts and almonds.

CONSTITUTION AND GOVERNMENT

Greece is a parliamentary democracy. Legislative power is exercised by parliament (the Vouli) and the president of the republic, who approves and promulgates the laws. All but 12 of the 300 members of parliament are elected by the people under a system of 'reinforced' proportional representation. The 12 State deputies are designated by the political parties in proportion to the number of votes cast for each party.

Executive power is exercised jointly by the president and the government. The president is elected by parliament for a term of five years. He appoints the prime minister and, on the latter's recommendation, the other ministers.

Greece is divided into 52 *nomói* (prefectures) and 13 regions: Eastern Macedonia and Thrace, Central Macedonia, Western Macedonia, Epirus, Thessaly, Western Greece, Central Greece, Attica, Peloponnese, Northern Aegean, Southern Aegean, Crete, and the Ionian Islands.

An elaborately decorated clock tower at Symi.
Fotostock

From ancient times, olives remain a staple product in Greece.
Fotostock

'What are the first five things that spring to mind when you think about Greece ?'

▶ Islands - Parthenon - Onassis - Moussaka - Socrates

Parthenon

The Parthenon is the temple situated on the hill of the Acropolis in Athens. The name Parthenon comes from the cult of Athena Parthenos (Athena the Virgin). The Athenian statesman, Pericles, directed its construction, and work began in 447 BC. The building itself was completed in 438 BC and work on the exterior decoration continued until 432 BC. Although the Parthenon has suffered damage over the centuries including the loss of many of its sculptures, it has retained the basic structure. Sculptures taken from the Parthenon can today be found, among other places, in London, Paris and Copenhagen.

Islands

There are over 2 000 islands scattered across the Aegean and Ionian seas which gives Greece a coastline of 15 021 km and explains why it is such a popular destination for beach and sun holidays. Tourism is a significant source of income for Greece and the problem of intense tourist concentration in a small number of resorts is lessened because of the islands. The islands, which account for approximately one fifth of the whole country's area, are generally subdivided into two groups. The Ionian islands, located to the west of the mainland which include Corfu, and the Aegean islands, located to the east which are much more numerous and include Rhodes and Crete. Only 136 of the islands are inhabited.

The beautiful island of Mykonos is a popular tourist destination.

Van Parys Media

Paschalidis

Onassis

Aristotle Onassis was a Greek shipping magnate and international businessman who developed a fleet of supertankers and freighters larger than the navies of many countries. He was born in 1906 to a family of wealthy tobacco dealers in Smyrna (now Turkish-owned Izmir). When the city was captured by the Turks in 1922, his family lost almost everything, but managed to send Aristotle to South America. It was there, working in a tobacco-importing business that he made his first small fortune. The Greek Government asked Onassis to negotiate a trade agreement with Argentina in 1928. He was then made Consul General. By the age of 25, Onassis had made his first million. He became involved in cigarette manufacturing and commodities trading. In 1932 he bought his first six freight ships. During the 1940s and 1950s his fleet of ships grew in size and his business empire flourished. From 1957 to 1974, he owned and managed the Greek national airline by concession from the government. He married Jacqueline Bouvier Kennedy, the widow of John F. Kennedy in 1968. He died in Paris in 1975.

Greece's coastal waters are superb for water sports.

Moussaka

Although it is most closely associated with Greece, moussaka is in fact a traditional dish of the whole Balkan area and the Middle East. In the Greek version, it is made with baked lamb and aubergine. The aubergines are sliced and fried in olive oil and then layered in a casserole dish with a mixture of ground lamb, onions, tomato sauce, and seasonings. A béchamel sauce with grated cheese is then poured over the meat and vegetables and the dish is ready for baking in the oven. Sliced potatoes are sometimes placed in the bottom of the casserole dish to form a bottom layer.

EKA

Socrates

Socrates was an ancient Greek philosopher who attempted to analyse the character of human life. He is remembered for his instruction to 'know thyself' and is credited with a major contribution to philosophical thought. Socrates was born in 470 BC in Athens. A major figure of the city in his time, he held discussions with politicians, poets and artisans about morals and paths through life. Most controversial were his conversations with young scholars, whom he encouraged to question life, their notions of themselves and beliefs about right and wrong. In 399 BC he was indicted for 'impiety' on two counts, 'corruption of the young' and 'neglect of the gods whom the city worships and the practice of religious novelties'. He was found guilty and sentenced to death by poisoning. Although offered a chance to escape, he refused and took the deadly potion. One of the extraordinary things about Socrates is that he never actually wrote anything. Most, if not all the information we have about him is found in the dialogues of Plato and the *Memorabilia* of Xenophon. Socrates, Plato and Aristotle, all part of the Greek philosophical tradition are recognized as three of the most influential philosophers of western civilization.

Athens University. From ancient times to the present day, Athens has been a seat of learning.

EKA

SPAIN

The Expo '92 in Seville showed the world the modern face of Spain, 500 years after Columbus sailed to America.
Isopress

POPULATION
39 million

CAPITAL
Madrid

★

1986

W—E

Spain is the most mountainous country in Europe after Switzerland: mountain ranges alternate with river basins to provide the great scenic variety of the Spanish landscape. The highest mountain peak is the Teide (3 718 m) on the island of Tenerife, which is one of the Canary archipelago. The longest river is the Ebro (910 km) which flows into the Mediterranean.

LAND

Spain has an area of 504 800 km². The Balearic Islands in the Mediterranean Sea and the Canary Islands in the Atlantic Ocean are integral parts of the country, which also includes some small areas in north Africa, on the peninsular coast which lies 30 km to the south. Mainland Spain is bordered by France to the north and Portugal to the west.

PEOPLE

Spain has a population of 39 million and an average population density of 78 inhabitants per km². With a population of almost 5 million, the autonomous community of Madrid has the greatest population density. In fact with the exception of Madrid, there has been a growing tendency for the population to concentrate on the coastal regions and actual depopulation in the interior due to industrialization and urbanization. Between 1960 and 1977 it is estimated that approximately 2.5 million Spaniards emigrated to other western countries. Many of them returned, however, after several years abroad. Of the 485 000 foreign residents, over half of them are from EU countries, in particular the United Kingdom (86 000), Portugal (38 000) and Germany (50 000).

The principal language is Castilian Spanish. Catalan, Basque and Galician are officially recognized in their respective autonomous communities.

ECONOMY

Spain is one of the world's largest exporters of cars. Other important industries are shipbuilding, chemicals, steel, textiles and footwear. Fifty-four per cent of the land surface is used for agriculture. The principal crops include citrus fruits, grapes and olives; wine and olive oil are important products. Fishing is also an significant industry, the Spanish fleet being one of the largest in the world. The tourism industry makes a considerable contribution to the Spanish economy.

CONSTITUTION AND GOVERNMENT

Spain is a constitutional hereditary monarchy and parliamentary democracy under the constitution of 1978.

The King is head of State and commander-in-chief of the armed forces.

Parliament (the Cortes Generales) consists of two houses: the Congress of Deputies (Lower House), made up of 350 members returned by direct universal suffrage in provincial elections (proportional representation), and the Senate (Upper House), composed of 225 senators elected in each of the provinces or appointed by the legislatures of the autonomous communities. Legislation is normally adopted by both houses, but the final decision lies with the Congress if there is a failure to agree.

Elections take place every four years. Since 1983 there are 17 autonomous regions in Spain, each with its own parliament and executive. These are Andalusia, Aragon, Asturias, the Balearic Islands, the Canary Islands, Cantabria, Castile and Leon, Castile-La Mancha, Catalonia, Extremadura, Galicia, Madrid, Murcia, Navarre, La Rioja, Valencia and the Basque Country. Ceuta and Melilla have special status.

The Alfonso XII Monument, Retiro Park, Madrid.
Isopress

The champion cyclist Miguel Indurain wearing the yellow jersey during the 1995 Tour de France.
Isopress

'What are the first five things that spring to mind when you think about Spain?'

▶ Barcelona - Paella - Bullfighting - Art - Juan Carlos

Barcelona

Barcelona is the capital of Barcelona province and of the autonomous region of Catalonia. It is Spain's major Mediterranean port and commercial centre. The main axis of the old town is formed by the Ramblas, a series of broad tree-lined avenues, leading from the commercial centre, Plaça de Catalunya to the seafront. Pavement artists, buskers, tarot card readers, and market stalls catering to every taste, can be found here. Barcelona can be divided into two artistic sectors. The Gothic quarter contains the Cathedral, the Church of Santa Maria del Mar, the City Hall and the seat of the autonomous government of Catalonia, the Palau de la Generalitat. The other major architectural influence in Barcelona is the work of modernist architect Antoni Gaudi. The Cathedral of the Sagrada Familia and the Parc Güell are two of his most remarkable achievements. In the years leading up to the 1992 Olympic games, Barcelona underwent major refurbishment especially in the port area where an Olympic village for 15 000 people was developed. By the year 2000, Barcelona hopes to have established itself as a major financial centre and work is presently under way to realize this dream.

Barcelona's famous Casa Batilo by Antoni Gaudi.

Fotostock

ress

Paella

A Spanish dish originating from the rice-growing areas on Spain's Mediterranean coast, paella is especially associated with the region of Valencia. The name comes from the utensil in which it is cooked, a flat round pan with two handles, although in the region it is simply known as *arroz* (rice). Traditionally, paella is cooked out in the open over a wood fire. Paella normally consists of saffron-flavoured rice cooked with seafood and vegetables. Meats such as chicken, pork or rabbit are also used and are cut into small pieces and sautéed with the seafood in olive oil, onions, garlic and herbs. Rice, tomatoes, saffron and stock are simmered together and then the meats and seafood are mixed in. The dish is garnished with peas, peppers and other vegetables.

The Basque country of north-eastern Spain has a high reputation for its cuisine.

Bullfighting

This old and symbolic ritual of man and beast has its roots in ancient cultures. Its first graphic representations can be found in Crete. Bullfighting has been extremely popular in Spain since the late 16th century. It was said to represent the triumph of the common man (*torero*, on foot) over the feudal knight (*picador*, on horseback). The *corrida* was a part of most popular feasts, and the *toro de lidia* (bull bred for bullfighting) has now become a part of the Spanish landscape. Goya and Picasso engravings, Bizet music and Hemingway writings have made the *corrida* well known out of Spain.

Art

Some of the most celebrated names in modern art are Spanish. Picasso has been called the most famous painter this century. Like his fellow countrymen, Miró, Dali and the architect Gaudi, he challenges the viewer's traditional view of life and art. All four had an extremely personal style that often involved vivid colours and dreamlike surrealist images, yet they are the inheritors of a rich cultural tradition. In the case of Dali and Picasso there existed a fascination with the monstrous. Along with Miró they were also interested in and became famous for their sculpture. All these artists spent some of their lives in or near Barcelona and as a result much of their work can be seen there.

Isopress

Picasso amongst some of his works.

Isopress

Juan Carlos

The King of Spain since 1975, Juan Carlos de Borbon y Borbon spent his early years in Italy and Portugal and first came to Spain in 1947. He was married to Princess Sophia of Greece in 1962 in Athens. They have two daughters, Elena and Christina and a son Felipe. In 1981 Juan Carlos became the first Spanish king to visit America and the first monarch to make an official visit to China. The Spanish people hold their royal family in high regard. The amount of respect and admiration the King enjoys today is not merely due to his role in the consolidation of Spanish democracy but also to the simple and unsophisticated lifestyle he and his family lead.

Spain's royal family at Palma de Mallorca.

The Lyons Opera, recently redesigned by the architect Jean Nouvel, illustrates how tradition and modernity can be combined in French design.
Van Parys Media

FRANCE

POPULATION
57 million

CAPITAL
Paris

★

Founding member

France offers a wide variety of landscape and scenery — the natural frontiers of the Pyrenees, the western Alps, the Jura and the Vosges, the plains of Beauce and Brie and the Causses plateaux. The highest mountain is Mont Blanc which reaches 4 807 m and the longest river is the Loire at 1 020 km.

LAND

The French Republic is situated in western Europe. It is bordered to the east by Belgium, Luxembourg, Germany, Switzerland and Italy and to the south by Spain. The English Channel lies to the north, the Mediterranean to the south and the Atlantic ocean to the west. The total land area is 544 000 km² including the island of Corsica, an integral part of the country.

Like Paris, France possesses a rich historical and cultural heritage. Its 30 000 listed historic buildings and monuments include Romanesque churches, Gothic cathedrals and Renaissance chateaux.

PEOPLE

France has a population of 57.3 million and an average population density of 105.5 people per km². Paris, the capital, has a population of over 2 million, with Greater Paris supporting a population of 8 million. Foreign residents account for 6.3% of the population, and of the 1.3 million migrant workers from countries within the Union, almost half are Portuguese. Algerians form the second largest foreign community, followed by Moroccans.

The official language of the Republic is French.

One of France's high-speed rail lines, the TGV Atlantique.
Michel Henri — SNCF CAV

ECONOMY

France is the largest agricultural country in Western Europe and, after Italy, the world's biggest producer of wine. It is also one of the world's leading industrial countries, prominent in the areas of steel production, cars and aerospace. The main industrial centres lie near Paris, in the north-east, in Lorraine and around Lyons.

CONSTITUTION AND GOVERNMENT

France is a republic in which, under the constitution, power is shared between the president, the government and the National Assembly. The president is elected directly by the people for a term of seven years. He is the Head of State and appoints the prime minister. He appoints or dismisses other ministers on the prime minister's recommendation and presides over the Council of Ministers. He can also dissolve the National Assembly and submit major bills to a referendum. The government, according to the constitution, 'determines and conducts the policy of the nation'.

Parliament consists of two chambers: the National Assembly and the Senate. The 577 members of the National Assembly are elected from departmental lists by a two-ballot system. The 317 senators are elected by indirect suffrage for a term of nine years by an electoral college made up of the deputies, the general (departmental) councillors, the mayors and municipal councillors. One third of the Senate is renewed every three years. Bills pass through both chambers. In the event of a disagreement a joint committee is set up to produce a common text; if the committee cannot agree, the government can seek a final decision from the National Assembly. The government is responsible to the National Assembly.

Metropolitan France is divided into 22 regions and 95 departments. There are four overseas departments (French Guiana, Guadeloupe, Martinique and Réunion), four overseas territories (French Polynesia, French Southern and Antarctic Territories, New Caledonia, and the Wallis and Futuna Islands) and two *collectivités territoriales* Mayotte, and Saint Pierre and Miquelon).

'What are the first five things that spring to mind when you think about France ?'

▶ Wine - Paris - Gérard Depardieu - Food - Fashion

A. Guilhem-Ducleon — CIVB

Wine

France is one of the world's leading wine producers, and the French are very proud of their wines. There are 300 varieties of grapes used in the making of French wine. Most are grown in southern France. Half of the total production, designated for daily consumption, comes from the six departments in the south and south-east. Grapes for high quality wine come from several different regions including; Alsace, Bordeaux, Burgundy, Champagne and the Loire valley. Often the wine is aged, sometimes for many years in deep cellars or caves.

The grape harvest in Bordeaux.

Paris

The capital of France is located in the north-central part of the country, on both sides of the river Seine. The oldest part is the Île de la Cité, where the magnificent Notre Dame cathedral is situated. The Place de la Bastille, on the right bank of the Seine, was the scene of the capture of the Bastille which started the French Revolution on 14 July 1789. Paris is home to some of the world's most celebrated museums. The Louvre has one of the largest and most impressive art collections in the world which includes one of Paris' best known inhabitants — the *Mona Lisa*. Other notable museums include the Musée d'Orsay for 19th century art and the National Museum of Modern Art in the Pompidou Centre. The tree-lined Champs-Elysées leads up to the Arc de Triomphe, which was commissioned by Napoleon in 1806. This and the Eiffel Tower have become symbols of France. The city has always been renowned for its nightlife and Montmartre is still the centre of nocturnal activity with its many cafes and bistros.

The Louvre pyramid.

Rollerskating on the Esplanade du Trocadéro.

Marc Vertille

B. Barbier — Sygma

Gérard Depardieu

The internationally famous French actor arrived in Paris at the age of 17, and a few years later he received his first training in acting at the Théâtre National Populaire. In 1974 he starred in his first successful film *Going places* in which he played a likeable thug, and 1978 saw him go to Cannes when the film in which he was starring, *Rêve de singe* (*Bye-bye monkey*), a futuristic fable filmed in New York, won the acclaimed special Grand Jury prize. *Jean de Florette* opened in 1986 to international acclaim. A further highly successful film was *Cyrano de Bergerac*, released the same year that saw Depardieu in his first English speaking role — *Green card* (1990).

Scene from the film *Cyrano de Bergerac* (1990)
by Jean-Paul Rappeneau, starring Gérard Depardieu.

Isopress

Food

Cooking is considered an art by the French. They are world famous for the diversity and sophistication of their cuisine. Almost every region, city and restaurant of France has its own food speciality. Some unusual specialities are snails and frogs legs in the Burgundy region. Others include charcuterie in Lyon, ommelettes (crêpes and galettes) in Brittany, and cassoulet, foie gras and truffles (mushroom-like plants) from the south-west. France produces over 300 different types of cheese, the most popular of which are Brie, Camembert and Roquefort. While it has now become possible to buy a baguette or croissant in supermarkets all over Europe, the French enjoy a wide variety of pastries and bread and prefer to buy it from the boulangerie-pâtisserie.

Delicious food, beautifully presented distinguishes French gastronomy.

Catherine Thibault

Fashion

Coco Chanel is possibly the most important name in the history of fashion. The French fashion designer who presided over Parisian haute couture for almost 60 years started off with a tiny millinery shop in Deauville in 1913. Her elegant yet simple styles were attractive to women at the time used to uncomfortable, complicated and corseted clothes. At the height of her career, the Chanel empire employed 3 500 people and included a fashion house, a textile business and perfume laboratories. Many young designers flocked to Paris to learn from the great master and France's reputation as a fashion mecca developed. During the 1960s, there was a rapid worldwide expansion of the fashion industry. France exported selected original designs to manufacturers abroad. They were then copied and mass-produced locally. Today the Paris fashion shows are still the most prestigious and French designers enjoy international success. Meanwhile Chanel's classic designs never seem to lose their popularity.

IRELAND/ÉIRE

The Financial Services Centre
by the river Liffey in Dublin.
Bord Failte Photo

Trinity College, Dublin has a world-
class academic record.
Eureka Slide

POPULATION
3 547 000

CAPITAL
Dublin

★
1973

*Ireland consists of 26 of
the 32 counties on the
island of Ireland. The
remaining six counties, in
the north, form Northern
Ireland, which is part of
the United Kingdom.
Ireland lies in the Atlantic
Ocean, about 80 km west
of Great Britain.
The nearest country to its
west is the United States
of America.*

LAND

The total area of Ireland is 70 284 km². This comprises a large central lowland of limestone with a relief of hills and a number of coastal mountains, the highest of which is Carrantuohill at 1 040 m. The Shannon is the longest river and there are many lakes. The country is divided into four provinces; Ulster, Munster, Leinster and Connaught. Dublin, the capital, is in Leinster and is situated on the east coast at the mouth of the river Liffey.

PEOPLE

The population of Ireland has been on the increase since 1961 and is now approximately 3.5 million, 1 million of whom live in the greater Dublin area. The population density is 50.4 inhabitants per km². Ireland has some 88 000 foreign residents (1991), 68 000 of whom come from other Community countries, particularly the United Kingdom. The rate of emigration is the highest in Europe. The number of Irish-born people living outside their native land is estimated at half the population of the country.

The Irish constitution recognizes Irish (Gaelic) as the first language and official documents are published in both English and Irish. The use of Irish as a vernacular is, however, limited to certain areas known as the Gaeltacht. English is the mother tongue of almost all the population.

O'Connell Street, Dublin,
one of the 'fair city's' main streets.
Fotostock

ECONOMY

The Irish economy is very open. With a domestic market of only 3.5 million people it is heavily dependent on trade; exports of goods and services alone amount to almost 80% of GNP. The rapid pace of development and industrialization in recent decades has been due in large measure to policies designed to make Ireland an attractive location for overseas investment. Forbairt is the agency responsible for developing indigenous industry while the Industrial Development Agency (IDA Ireland) encourages outside investment, particularly in new technology. Agriculture and tourism are important parts of the economy.

CONSTITUTION AND GOVERNMENT

Ireland is a parliamentary democracy. Legislative power is vested in the Oireachtas (National Parliament), which consists of the President of Ireland and two houses, namely Dáil Éireann (House of Representatives) and Seanad Éireann (Senate). For the Dáil, 166 members are elected directly for a maximum period of five years under a system of proportional representation. Of the 60 senators elected for the same period, 11 are nominated by the Taoiseach (prime minister), 43 are elected by members of the Dáil, the previous Seanad and by the local authorities from panels of candidates from five key sectors of society: education, agriculture, labour, industry and commerce, and administration, and six are elected by the country's university graduates.

Bills which would alter the constitution are required to be passed by both chambers and endorsed by a referendum of the electorate. The president, elected for a seven-year term, appoints the Taoiseach on the nomination of the Dáil, and the other ministers on the advice of the Taoiseach and with the prior approval of the Dáil. Dáil Éireann is summoned and dissolved by the president on the advice of the Taoiseach. There may be up to 15 members in the government, of whom two may be nominated from the Senate whilst the remainder must be members of the Dáil.

'What are the first five things that spring to mind when you think about Ireland?'

▶ Green - Pubs - Celtic design - James Joyce - U2

Inpho/Lorraine O'Sullivan

Green

Ireland is also poetically known as the 'Emerald Isle' and most of the tourists come to Ireland in the hope of seeing the beautiful green landscapes. No part of Ireland is more than 110 km from the sea and this combined with the high precipitation rates means that the grass is indeed very green. Less than one eighth of the land is actually arable. It is, however, highly fertile and 81% of the total land area is used for agriculture, predominantly grassland pasture. Many people associate the colour green with Ireland because of 'The boys in green', namely Ireland's national football team, who wear green shirts. Green is also the colour worn traditionally on St Patrick's Day, 17 March (Ireland's national holiday) which honours the saint thought to have brought Christianity to Ireland.

Jason Sherlock is fast becoming one of Ireland's most famous sports personalities. Sherlock, who hails from Dublin is one of an increasing band of Irish youngsters who combine Ireland's previously parochial national sport, Gaelic football, with the more internationally renowned soccer. During the summer 1995 All Ireland Gaelic Football Championship, Sherlock set the unusual precedent by becoming the sport's first real celebrity. Great natural sporting ability combined with a worry-free demeanour of one so young has given Sherlock something of a pop star status throughout Ireland.

The Irish pub

In Ireland the pub has always been a focus of social life. The 'pub culture' which has developed means that drinking habits in Ireland differ from the wine-drinking countries of the Mediterranean. Beer accounts for two thirds of all alcohol consumed and this will generally be consumed in a pub while socializing. Pubs in Ireland are only licensed to stay open till 11 p.m. in the winter and 11.30 p.m. in the summer. Contrary to popular belief, less alcohol is consumed in Ireland than in other European countries. It has now become commonplace to find an Irish pub in many European cities. This is in part due to the number of expatriates living abroad, but also due to the reputation of having a friendly ambience and good live music.

Live folk music helps to keep Irish pub culture thriving.

Isopres

Eureka Slide

Celtic design

For many centuries Ireland has been enriched by its people's instinct for design, and craftsmanship. The Tara brooch, dating from the mid-eighth century is an exquisite example of metalworking technique, and *The Book of Kells*, an illuminated manuscript of the four Gospels, is another medieval treasure of calligraphic design. Traditional materials and techniques are still used in Irish design today. The contemporary clothes designer John Rocha, who has been based in Dublin for the past 16 years, has the philosophy 'to use traditional cloths, but with a new, modern feel'. His flair for combining old and new, local tweed from Donegal and linen, and the vibrant colours and intricate tailoring of modern design, has earned him international renown.

James Joyce

James Augustine Aloysius Joyce was born in Dublin in 1882 and died in Zurich in 1941. He is noted for his experimental use of language and new literary methods. His most well-known works are *Dubliners* (1914), *A portrait of the artist as a young man* (1916), *Ulysses* (1922), and *Finnegans Wake* (1939). In general, it is widely accepted that literature by Irish authors has profoundly influenced the whole of English literature. Writers such as Jonathan Swift, Edmund Burke, William Butler Yeats, Oscar Wilde, George Bernard Shaw, and Samuel Beckett are all part of the English-speaking Irish literary tradition. In 1995, the poet Seamus Heaney became the fourth Irishman to win the Nobel prize for literature.

Van Parys Media

U2

Probably Ireland's most famous rock export. The band consisting of Bono, The Edge, Adam Clayton, and Larry Mullen Jnr formed in 1977 after Larry put a notice up at school about starting a band. They have soared to international fame since then. They had an audience of 400 people at their first public concert in Dublin in 1979 and an audience of 65 000 people at a concert in Marseilles in 1993. *The Joshua tree* is their biggest album success to date, reaching number one in the UK and USA in 1987.

The supergroup U2, at the 1995 MTV music awards.

POPULATION
56.9 million

CAPITAL
Rome

★

Founding member

The Appenine mountain range extends almost the entire length of Italy, the highest mountain being the Gran Sasso (2 914 m). The longest river is the Po (652 km), which rises in the Cottian Alps and flows through the delta-like estuary into the Adriatic Sea. Italy is home to Europe's largest volcano. Mount Etna is situated on the island of Sicily and reaches 3 262 m. Although it erupts periodically, the area is heavily populated because the volcanic ash makes the soil fertile.

ITALY

LAND

The Italian Republic comprises a peninsula, extending from southern Europe into the Mediterranean Sea, and a number of islands. The two main islands are Sicily to the south-west and Sardinia to the west. The Alps form a natural frontier to the north with France, Switzerland, Austria and Slovenia. The independent Republic of San Marino and the Vatican City State lie within Italian State territory.

PEOPLE

Italy has a population of almost 57 million and an average population density of 189 people per km². Rome is the most densely populated city with 2.7 million people. Of its 781 000 foreign residents, 150 000 come from other countries within the Union, predominantly Germany, the United Kingdom and France. Immigration from third world countries is a recent phenomenon.

The national language is Italian; other languages spoken include German (in Alto Adige), French (Valle d'Aosa), Slovene (Trieste and Gorizia) and Ladin (some areas of the Alto Adige).

ECONOMY

Over recent decades Italy has developed from an agricultural to an industrial country. The pace of economic development has not, however, been uniform throughout the country and there are still significant differences between north and south. Italy's principal exports include machinery and transport equipment, chemicals, clothing and footwear. Tourism remains a significant source of income.

CONSTITUTION AND GOVERNMENT

Italy is a parliamentary republic. Power is vested in parliament, which consists of the Chamber of Deputies and the Senate, both of which have equal powers. The 630 deputies and 315 senators are elected for five years. Under a statute enacted in August 1993, 75% of the deputies are chosen by a simple majority in single-member constituencies and 25% by proportional representation. Senators are elected regionally. The president, who is elected by parliament, appoints the president of the Council of Ministers (prime minister) and, on the latter's recommendation, the other ministers, promulgates laws and may send back laws enacted by parliament for reconsideration.

For administrative purposes, Italy is divided into 20 regions, with considerable autonomy. Five of them — Valle d'Aosta, Trentino-Alto Adige, Sicily, Sardinia and Friuli-Venezia Giuila — have special constitutions giving them a wider degree of autonomy than the other 15.

The snow-clad Dolomites of north-eastern Italy.
Van Parys Media

The Italian football superstar, Dino Baggio.
Isopress

A superb example of Sicilian baroque architecture.
Uwe Wissenbach

'What are the first five things that spring to mind when you think about Italy ?'

▶ Rome - Pasta - Shoes - Art - Pavarotti

Isopress

Rome

Rome is the capital of Italy and one of the world's greatest historic cities. For hundreds of years, Rome was the supreme power of Europe, northern Africa, and western Asia. Rome lies on the banks of the Tiber river in central Italy. Ancient Rome was built on seven hills. Today the city encompasses about 20. The Colosseum, a huge half-ruined amphitheatre, is one of the chief landmarks. The Vatican City, in the centre of Rome is home to St Peter's Church, the world's largest Christian church and an impressive example of Renaissance architecture. The Trevi fountain, completed in 1762, is very popular with tourists as it is said that visitors who throw coins into the fountain will someday return to the city. It also features in a famous scene from the Italian director, Frederico Fellini's film *La dolce vita*. Throughout Rome there are many beautiful squares connected by busy streets. The heart of Rome and its commercial centre is around the Piazza Colonna. People-watching is a popular occupation here as Romans and visitors alike sit in outdoor cafes or stroll through some of the open-air markets.

Rome's Trevi fountain.

The Colosseum.

The famous Trevi fountain scene from Fellini's masterful film, *La dolce vita*.

Pasta

It is said that pasta was first brought to Italy by the ancient Greeks. The first form was called *makaria*, which is probably what we now know as macaroni. There are an estimated 400 known shapes in existence and a Spaghetti Historical Museum in Pontedassio shows the history of the food. This all aside, however, pasta is not the staple diet of the Italians as is popularly portrayed. As in many other European countries, each region has its own culinary speciality. The sausages of Bologna, the prosciutto (salted ham) of Parma and the minestrone of Milan are just a few examples. Most Italians would not order pasta when they go out to eat but take advantage of some of the finest fruits, vegetables or seafood Europe has to offer, within their own country.

Van Parys Media

Fotostock

Shoes

Italians have a reputation for being stylish and well-dressed. Indeed they spend more on clothes and shoes than any of the other 14 members of the EU. In fact it amounts to 10% of their total expenditure. It is no surprise then perhaps, that these industries are so important to their economy. Italy is Europe's largest producer of shoes, and the world's second largest (behind China). Coupled to this, is the industry's reputation for quality and design. Shoes from Italy have a cachet that cannot be matched by any other country. Perhaps this is in part a reflection of how the Italian shoe industry operates. Traditionally, most firms are small and family run. Until recently, the Gucci firm were a perfect example of this. Their company was set up by Maurizo Gucci in Florence at the turn of the century, and it has grown and diversified ever since. Its famous loafers were worn by the likes of Jackie Kennedy and Grace Kelly in the 1960s, and in the 1980s the firm reiterated its old philosophy of craftsmanship and quality to a new generation, and is enjoying continued success today.

Art

Italy was the birthplace of some of the greatest names in art and sculpture. Italian artists played important roles in early Christian art and in the styles of the Middle Ages. Giotto, an artist of the early Renaissance, was part of a revolutionary movement in painting which began showing the human body as three dimensional and did not limit the subject matter to merely religious themes. Renaissance painters such as Leonardo da Vinci, Michelangelo, Raphael and Boticelli also made their works more realistic and introduced changes in the use of colour. Many of Michelangelo's greatest paintings decorate the ceiling and front wall of the Vatican's Sistine Chapel. He is widely regarded as the most eminent artist of the Renaissance. Among the best-known modern Italian artists are the painters Giorgio de Chirico and Amedeo Modigliani and the sculptors Giacomo Manzù and Marino Marini. Every year, countless visitors come to Italy to see some of the priceless art collections and magnificent architecture, Rome and Florence being the two most popular destinations.

Florence, campanile and cathedral (Duomo).

A detail from the Boticelli painting *The birth of Venus*, at the Uffizi Gallery in Florence.

EKA

Pavarotti

Pavarotti has become one of the most famous international opera stars this century. He has also helped to revive its popularity. Born in Modena, Italy in 1935, Luciano Pavarotti made his professional debut in Reggio nell' Emilia in 1961. He is widely admired for the warmth and flexibility of his voice, the security of his high notes and the intensity of emotion in his singing. Pavarotti has concentrated almost entirely on Italian operas and songs and his most popular song to date is a version of *Nessun Dorma*. One of the best-selling classical music albums of all time is a recording of the 1994 concert in Los Angeles given by Pavarotti, José Carreras and Placido Domingo — 'The three tenors'.

LUXEMBOURG

The wine-growing valley of the Moselle river.
EKA

Luxembourg is a strong financial centre.
Van Parys Media

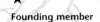

POPULATION

400 900

CAPITAL

City of Luxembourg

★

Founding member

LAND

The Grand Duchy of Luxembourg is a land-locked country in western Europe. It has an area of 2 586 km² and is bordered by Belgium to the west and north, by France to the south, and by Germany to the east. The main topographical features of the country are the Oesling, a 450 m high plateau which is part of the Ardennes, and the Gutland, which rises to an average height of 250 m. The main rivers are the Moselle, the Our and the Sûre.

PEOPLE

Luxembourg has a population of 400 900 with an average population density of 148 inhabitants per km². Luxembourg's population comprises a mixture of ethnic groups. While the French, German and Belgians predominate, Italians and Portuguese account for a significant minority of the population. Over 30% of the population are foreigners.

'Lëtzebuergesch' is the spoken language and became an official language in 1984. French is generally used for administrative purposes and German tends to be the main written language of the press.

ECONOMY

Luxembourg has a developed market economy largely based on heavy industries, international trade and banking. The Luxembourg steel industry is among the strongest steel industries in Europe and the western world. Manufacturing industries constitute the most important sector of the economy, contributing over a quarter of the GDP in 1990. Luxembourg's most important trading partners are Belgium, Germany and France.

CONSTITUTION AND GOVERNMENT

Luxembourg is a representative democracy and constitutional monarchy. Executive power lies with the Grand Duke. It is exercised by the members of the government under the coordinating authority of the prime minister. The Chamber of Deputies represents the nation. The deputies are elected by the people.

The Grand Duke and the Chamber of Deputies can both initiate legislation. The Chamber examines and debates bills laid before it, and passes or rejects them by vote. No final vote may be taken on bills until the Council of State has delivered an opinion. The functions of the Council of State under the constitution are to consider bills and amendments referred to it, to settle administrative disputes and to give opinions on any other matters referred to it by the Grand Duke or under the law. Luxembourg is divided into 12 cantons.

La Corniche in the city of Luxembourg.

SIT Luxembourg

'What are the first five things that spring to mind when you think about Luxembourg ?'

▶ Castles – Banks – Court of Justice – Small – Echternach dancing procession

Castles

In December 1994, the World Heritage Committee of Unesco decided to include the old town and fortifications of Luxembourg in its famous list of world cultural monuments. The name Luxembourg, derived from the word *Lucilinburugh,* means 'little fortress' and the city of Luxembourg is characterized by its military architecture. Occupations by different foreign forces — Burgundy, Spain, France, Austria, and Prussia — helped to give the city its present structure and form. Each successive occupant built up the fortress to make it the strongest in Europe after Gibraltar. Although much of the fortress was dismantled in 1867, there is still enough of it there to leave a striking impression on any visitor.

Clervaux.

Van Parys Media

Banks

Between 1970 and 1990, the number of banking houses and their employees in Luxembourg, increased fourfold. Luxembourg has developed a financial centre that operates on a worldwide scale. A policy of banking secrecy exists, alongside one of the world's most severe legislations regarding drugs money laundering. Luxembourg's geographical situation and the prevailing constructive attitudes of the government, have further attracted investors. The banks have played an important role in Luxembourg's economic development, providing security for 15% of the country's gross national product. They also employ a large number of the working population and generate nearly a fifth of total tax revenue. The European Investment Bank, created in 1958 by the Treaty of Rome, has been based in Luxembourg since 1968.

Court of Justice

The Court of Justice of the European Communities serves to ensure that the implementation of the Treaties is in accordance with the rule of law. It is composed of 15 judges appointed for six years by agreement among the governments. They are assisted by nine advocates-general. The building of the Court of Justice, inaugurated in January 1973, stands on the Kirchberg plateau in Luxembourg. The conception was decided jointly by three young architects, two Belgian and one from Luxembourg, who were awarded prizes by an international jury at an architectural competition. The building has five floors and covers an area of 10 000 m². Other European institutions located in Luxembourg are the European Court of Auditors, the General Secretariat of the European Parliament, the Translation Centre for bodies of the European Union and several important services of the European Commission, including the Statistical Office (Eurostat) and the Publications Office as well as the Nuclear Safety Administration and the Directorate-General for Credit and Investments.

SIT Luxembourg

Small

Luxembourg is indeed a very small country. With a total land area of 2 586 km², the longest north-south axis measures 82 km and the maximum width of the country is just 57 km. Many analogies are made to illustrate Luxembourg's small size — the army is made up of about 700 volunteers including the military band. Luxembourgers are proud of their independent State with its own customs, language, high standard of living and low level of unemployment. Luxembourg has done well to remain independent considering that throughout its history the country has been besieged and occupied more than 20 times.

The Adolphe bridge, Luxembourg.

The Echternach dancing procession

Each year on Whit-Tuesday, a mysterious religious ceremony dating back to the Middle Ages takes place in the small fortified former abbey town of Echternach. Beginning from the abbey court at a quarter past nine, groups of pilgrims take to the street and perform a ritual dance. Rows of five dancers, holding white handkerchiefs between them, hop from foot to foot, sometimes crossing their legs while jumping, taking about an hour to cover a distance of a kilometre. It is performed in homage to Saint Willibrord (658-739), a missionary who by the end of his life had performed many miracles, and received both papal and royal favours. Today, the ceremony is as popular as ever, being something of a tourist attraction, as well as the uplifting religious celebration for both young and old that it has always been.

J. Picard

A traditional Dutch cheese
market in Alkmaar.
Fotostock

THE NETHERLANDS

POPULATION

15 million

CAPITAL

Amsterdam

★

Founding member

*The Netherlands has a
total land area of
41 526 km². The name
Holland is frequently
used instead of the
Netherlands, but this
actually refers to
the western coastal
provinces, North and
South Holland, which
have played an important
part in the country's
history. It is not
the correct name for
the whole country.*

LAND

The Netherlands is situated in the lowlands of
north-west Europe, bordered to the east by
Germany and to the south by Belgium. To the
north and west lies the North Sea. Just beyond
the coast lie the polders — land reclaimed from
the sea. Much of the country is below sea level
and the land is criss-crossed by lakes, rivers and
canals. Uplands are only found in the south-east.
The highest point is the Vaalserberg which
reaches a height of 321 metres.

PEOPLE

The Netherlands has a population of over 15
million with an average population density of
452 people per km², making it one of the most
densely populated countries in the world. The
most densely populated area is the Randstad
conurbation in the west of the country, which
centres around the cities of Amsterdam, The
Hague, Rotterdam and Utrecht. In the years after
the Second World War up to about 1960, there
were more people that emigrated from the
Netherlands than people that came to live there.
The situation has changed since then and the
number of foreign nationals settling in the
country has increased considerably over the
years. In 1995 there were 774 000 foreign
residents, 193 000 of whom came from other
countries within the Union, particularly Belgium.
Most of the foreign residents, however, come
from outside the Union, particularly from Turkey
and Morocco.

Dutch is the national language. In the north-east
of the country, in the province of Friesland, a
second official language is spoken, Frisian.

ECONOMY

The Netherlands' position in the heart of Europe
determines the character of the Dutch economy,
which is highly international in its orientation.
Trade and transport are two of its most
important sectors. In terms of cargo handled,
Rotterdam is the biggest port in the world. The
Netherlands has major chemical, electrical
engineering and car industries in addition to a
highly mechanized agricultural sector. Oil and
natural gas production are of considerable
economic importance.

CONSTITUTION AND GOVERNMENT

The Kingdom of the Netherlands is a
parliamentary democracy and hereditary
monarchy. The sovereign (the Queen) and the
cabinet together constitute the government.
Ministers are responsible to parliament (the
States-General), which consists of two chambers.
The 75 members of the Upper House are elected
indirectly by the provincial councils.
The 150 members of the Lower House are
elected directly, for four years, by a system of
proportional representation.

Bills may be introduced only by the government
or by members of the Lower House. The Upper
House has no right of amendment. The Council
of State advises on proposals for legislation.

The Netherlands is divided into 12 provinces:
Groningen, Flevoland, Friesland, Drenthe,
Overijssel, Gelderland, Utrecht, North Holland,
South Holland, Zeeland, North Brabant and
Limburg. Each province has a provincial council
and a provisional executive (responsible for day-
to-day business), both chaired by a Queen's
commissioner appointed by the government.

The royal palace, Amsterdam.
Eureka Slide

Rotterdam is the world's biggest
sea port and a city proud of its
futuristic architecture.
Eureka Slide

'What are the first five things that spring to mind when you think about the Netherlands ?'

▶ Van Gogh - Tulips - Amsterdam - Drugs - Flat

Eureka Slide

Van Gogh

Vincent van Gogh is generally considered to be the greatest Dutch painter after Rembrandt. He was a strong influence on the Expressionist movement in modern art, and his most famous pieces include *The potato eaters*, and *The sunflowers*. Many say that his striking use of colour, coarse brushwork and contoured forms show the anguish of his mental illness which eventually led to his suicide. During his lifetime Van Gogh completed more than 800 oil paintings and 700 drawings. He sold only one. In fact he lived in poverty for most of his life, sustained by his brother Theo. Born in Zundert, the Netherlands in 1853, Van Gogh died in 1890 in Auvers-sur-Oise two days after shooting himself.

Open air art: A reproduction of Van Gogh's 'self portrait' in a residential setting.

Tulips

The first Dutch tulips bloomed in the spring of 1594. They were planted by Carolus Clusius, the man in charge of the gardens at the University of Leiden. He had been given a handful of tulip bulbs by the Austrian Ambassador who had picked them during his diplomatic tenure in the Ottoman Empire. Tulips caused an instant sensation and soon became a sign of power and prestige for Dutch aristocrats. Today the tulip is the Netherlands' number one bulb export, followed by gladioli and iris. The largest flower auction house in the country is Verenigde Bloemenveilingen Aalsmeer, a cooperative of 5 000 growers. In fact, in terms of supply and turnover it is the largest auction of any kind, in the world. Nearly 14 million flowers and 1.5 million plants are sold at the Aalsmeer auction every weekday. The auction building itself is the size of 100 football fields. The Netherlands exports 59% of the world's cut flowers, primarily to Germany, France and the United Kingdom.

Isopress

Amsterdam

Although Amsterdam is the largest city and capital of the Netherlands, the seat of government is in The Hague, 55 km away. The name means 'dam of the Amstel' and refers to a dam built there during the 1200s. Four canals — the Singel, Herengracht, Keizersgracht and Prinsengracht border the old section of the city. This section has many beautiful buildings, some of which date back to the Middle Ages. The royal palace, built in the mid-1600s, overlooks Dam Square at the centre. The area contains a clutter of narrow streets and many are closed to traffic, except of course for bicycles which can be seen in abundance throughout the city.

Amsterdam's major cultural attractions include the Rijksmuseum, the Stedelijk museum of modern art and the Van Gogh museum. It is also home to the Anne Frank house, a municipal theatre and the world famous Concertgebouw Orchestra. Two universities make Amsterdam a lively student city with a buzzing and somewhat notorious nightlife.

By bicycle, the best way to get around Amsterdam's old narrow streets.

Eureka Slide

Drugs

Over 90% of the people asked, mentioned drugs as one of the five things they associated with the Netherlands. This reputation does not spring from the existence of an excessive drug problem, but because of the relatively relaxed rules that exist with regard to 'soft drugs'. The Netherlands was the first country in Europe to legalize the use of cannabis for personal use. (The actual legal amount is currently under discussion.) Some countries have followed suit or are currently debating whether to do so or not. Some 450 coffee shops in Amsterdam have been selling cannabis on a semi-legal basis since 1976. Advertising is not allowed and users must be over 18 years old. There are penalties for those caught dealing outside licensed premises. The coffee shops are tolerated by the police as it is felt that it is a way of containing and controlling the situation. According to a survey conducted in 1995 by the University of Rotterdam in the Netherlands, 82% of those questioned think that taking drugs is wrong, and 61% are in favour of a total ban; 40% support their tolerated sale in the coffee shops, and 37% are against this.

Flat

'God created the world, but the Dutch created Holland'. This old Dutch saying refers to the fact that approximately 40% of what is now the Netherlands, is land reclaimed from the sea, lakes and swamps. The drained areas are known as polders and are created by building a dike around the area and pumping the water into a series of canals. Much of the land is below sea level and therefore the Netherlands is indeed quite flat. The country has been plagued by flooding throughout its history and the Dutch have had to fight a constant battle against the sea. A statue in Spaarndam is inscribed in honour of the little Dutch boy, Hansje Brinker, whose actions have become a symbol of the eternal struggle against the sea. It is said that on his way home one evening he noticed water coming through a hole in the wall of one of the dikes. There was no one around he could tell and so he plugged the hole with his finger and waited until someone finally arrived the next day.

In cold winters, people can skate on the frozen drainage canal in Kinderdijk.

Isopress

AUSTRIA

Annaberg in Lammertal.
The beauty of Austria's mountains
change with the seasons.
Jezierzanski

🚶

POPULATION
7.8 million

🏛

CAPITAL
Vienna

★

1995

🧭

*Austria is the most
densely forested nation
in central Europe
(47% of its total land
area). The longest river
is the Danube which also
flows through Germany,
the Slovak Republic,
Hungary, Serbia and
Romania; 350 km of it
flows through Austria.*

LAND

The Republic of Austria lies in central Europe and is bordered by as many as eight countries: Switzerland and Liechtenstein to the west, Germany and the Czech Republic to the north, Hungary, and the Slovak Republic to the east and by Italy and Slovenia to the south. Its total land area is 83 857 km². It consists of nine federal States (Bundesländer): Vorarlberg, Tyrol, Salzburg, Upper Austria, Lower Austria, Vienna, Burgenland, Styria and Carinthia. Austria is a mountainous country where the Alps take up two thirds of the land area. The highest mountain is the Grossglockner at 3 797 m.

PEOPLE

The population of Austria is 7.8 million and has a minimal annual growth rate. Less than 20% of the population is younger than 15 years of age and more than 20% is over 60. The land is very unevenly populated. Almost 60% of the Alpine regions are sparsely populated and more than half the population live in Austria's cities. Vienna alone, has over 1.7 million inhabitants.

There are now approximately 300 000 foreigners living in Austria. Many work in the construction, tourism, and textile industries. Traditionally their lands of origin are Turkey or the former Yugoslavia. There is an ethnic group of Slovenes living in the province of Carinthia and smaller groups of Croats and Hungarians live in the province of Burgenland, all with their respective schools.

The national language is German and is said to be spoken in a softer, more drawling manner than in Germany.

ECONOMY

Austria is a highly developed industrial country with a free market economy. Foreign trade has always played an important role for the Austrian economy. Since the fall of the Iron Curtain, Austria's role as gateway to central and eastern European countries has increased considerably.

Roughly 40% of Austria's GNP is derived from commerce and foreign trade and services. After trade and industry, tourism — in summer as in winter — is one of the most developed branches of the economy.

CONSTITUTION AND GOVERNMENT

Austria is a democratic federal republic. At national level it is governed by a bicameral legislature. The lower house is called the National Council (Nationalrat). It has 83 members elected by popular vote on the basis of proportional representation. The upper house is called the Federal Council (Bundesrat) and has 63 members elected by the legislatures of the nine federal States (Bundesländer). It reviews and in some cases delays legislation passed by the Nationalrat (Parliament). The President of Austria is elected by popular vote for a term of six years. He appoints the chancellor from the party with the strongest representation or one of those able to form a coalition in the Nationalrat; he has the power to dissolve the parliament and is the supreme commander of the armed forces (Bundesheer).

This highly original
fresco extolling
the delights of
the famous
Austrian sausage,
can be found
at the Naschmarkt
in Vienna.
Uwe Wissenbach

Vienna.
Beckel

'What are the first five things that spring to mind when you think about Austria ?'

▶ Vienna - Klimt - Skiing - Sissi - Mozart

Isopress

Markowitsch

Vienna

Vienna is the capital city of Austria and also one of its nine Bundesländer. It has the smallest area but the largest population. For many centuries Vienna was the capital of the multinational Habsburg monarchy. Magnificent architecture, and museums and art galleries containing priceless treasures from virtually every period of western civilization reflect the splendour of the city's past. Renowned as a centre of European culture, Vienna is one of the most well-preserved of the great old European capitals. The city suffered extensive damage towards the end of World War II and there was much rebuilding. In spite of this, the character of Vienna as a whole is much the same as in the years before 1914 and it continues to be a world centre for music.

The highly decorated U-Bahn pavilion, Karlsplatz, Vienna.

One of Vienna's architectural delights, a house built between 1983 and 1985 to promote an ecological lifestyle, by the famous architect Hundertwasser.

Klimt

Gustav Klimt rebelled against academic art in favour of a highly decorative style, similar to art nouveau. He was born in Vienna in 1862 and died there in 1918. After studying at the Vienna School of Decorative Arts, Klimt opened his own studio specializing in the painting of murals. He later formed the Viennese Secession, an association which was to open Austrian art to innovation. This was an era in which Austrian painting achieved a position of international pre-eminence with painters such as Klimt, Schiele and Kokoschka coming to the fore. Their masterworks can be admired at the Österreichische Galerie in the Belvedere Castle in Vienna.

Fankhauser

Skiing

The fact that skiing is the most popular winter sport in Austria is partly due to the ideal topographical and climatic conditions which the country offers. But Austria has also played a leading role in the sport's development. As long ago as 1897 Matthias Zdarsky (1856-1940) wrote the world's first manual of skiing, invented the first viable ski binding and, in 1905, organized the first slalom race in skiing history. Toni Sailer, Karl Schranz, Annemarie Moser-Pröll, Franz Klammer are all names known throughout the skiing world. During the last quarter of a century, they and other Austrian skiers have won numerous Olympic gold medals and World Championship titles.

Skiing in the Tyrol.

Sissi

Sissi, or Elizabeth of Bavaria as is her official title, enjoys popularity largely due to the films of the same name starring Romy Schneider. The real Elizabeth was born in Munich in 1837, the daughter of Duke Maximilian Joseph. She was considered to be the most beautiful woman of her time and in 1854 she married Franz Joseph, Emperor of Austria and King of Hungary. They had a very stormy marriage. Although she distanced herself from direct involvement in her husband's politics, she had a profound influence on him. She was greatly in favour of the dual monarchy where Austria and Hungary existed in a sort of partnership and enjoyed the same status and rights. This made her very popular with the people. Franz Joseph was a disciplined traditionalist and found it hard to deal with his wife's contradictory, non-conformist character. While he admired her strength of character and courage, her refusal to conform to the ways of the Austrian court made her something of an outsider. After the suicide of her son, the Crown Prince Rudolf, she led a restless life involving a lot of travel. She was assassinated in Geneva by an Italian anarchist in 1898.

Mozart

Mozart is regarded as one of the greatest musical geniuses of all time. Born in Salzburg, Austria in 1756, he began to compose music when he was five years old. At the age of six he performed for the Empress Maria Theresa at the Schönbrunn Palace in Vienna. He was subsequently taken on a concert tour of Europe by his father which made him famous. While travelling, Mozart continued to compose. From 1775 to 1781, he was in the service of the Archbishop in Salzburg. After being dismissed in disgrace, Mozart produced his first mature opera *Idomeneo*. He then settled in Vienna and, after years of waiting, was employed by Emperor Joseph II as a chamber composer. During his time there he composed many of his most famous quartets, symphonies and operas including *The marriage of Figaro* (1786) and *Don Giovanni* (1787). Despite their success, Mozart's flamboyant lifestyle meant he fell further and further into debt. Neither his concert tour of 1789 nor the success of *Die Zauberflöte (The magic flute)* (1791) did anything to improve his financial situation. He died a poor man in 1791 in Vienna.

EKA

PORTUGAL

Fishing is a traditional industry for the Portuguese.
Isopress

Cultivation is possible in the mountains of Madeira, due to the island's man-made terraces.
Eureka Slide

POPULATION
9.8 million

CAPITAL
Lisbon

★
1986

Portugal offers a vast variety of landscapes. The river Tagus separates the mountainous north, which reaches a height of 1991 m in the Serra da Estrela, from the plains and plateaux of the south. The coast is marked by an alternation of fine sandy beaches and imposing rocky headlands. The main rivers of Portugal are the Tagus, the Douro and the Guadiana. The country's most important trading ports are Lisbon, Oporto and Setúbal.

LAND

The Portuguese Republic lies on the Atlantic side of the Iberian peninsula and includes archipelagos, the Azores and Madeira Islands in the Atlantic Ocean. Portugal is bordered by Spain to the north and east.

PEOPLE

The population of Portugal is 9.8 million, and it has an average population density of 107 people per km². There is, however, an irregular distribution pattern with a higher density in all the coastal area north of Lisbon. Lisbon and Oporto are the most densely populated cities. Between 1960 and 1972 alone, one and a half million people emigrated from Portugal. At that time, alongside economic reasons for leaving, the independence wars in former Portuguese colonies caused a considerable number of young men to leave the country in order to avoid military service. Today it is estimated that three million Portuguese are scattered around the globe — France, Germany and Luxembourg being important traditional destinations within the European Union.

The official language is Portuguese.

ECONOMY

Portugal has a small open economy, which is dependent on exports and imports. Its main European trading partners are Spain, the United Kingdom and Germany. The textile and clothing industry is the most important within the manufacturing sector, clothing alone accounting for an estimated 21.2% of total export earnings in 1992. During the post-accession years Portugal enjoyed Europe's highest growth rate. Foreign investment has helped to resuscitate the economy, and emigrants' remittances are also important. Industries traditionally associated with Portugal such as tourism and the production of port wine remain significant sources of income.

CONSTITUTION AND GOVERNMENT

Portugal is a parliamentary republic. Legislative power is exercised by parliament, which has one chamber of 230 deputies elected by direct universal suffrage for four years, using the d'Hondt system of proportional representation.

The President of the Republic is elected by direct universal suffrage for five years. Subject to the limitations imposed by the constitution, the president dissolves parliament, appoints the prime minister and dismisses the government.

Continental Portugal is divided into 18 districts. Each district has a civil governor, appointed by the government.

The Azores and Madeira are autonomous regions whose statutes provide for the election by direct universal suffrage of a Regional Assembly, to which a regional government with wide powers is responsible.

Van Parys Media

Lisbon has always had a nautical heritage.

'What are the first five things that spring to mind when you think about Portugal?'

▶ Port wine - Lisbon - Explorers - The Cock - Algarve

Van Parys Media

Port wine

Port wine began as an experiment to see what would happen to wine when brandy was added to it. (One rumour traces its origins to an abbot in a Lamego monastery.) Brandy halts fermentation which turns sugar into alcohol. By arresting this process, port retains a sweetness while the brandy strengthens the alcoholic content. The grape production and process are tightly regulated by the Port Wine Institute. Firstly the grapes must be grown in the Douro region, which according to the Institute, is the world's oldest demarcated wine region. Secondly, the grapes must be from a list of 15 red and 14 white recommended varieties and finally the port must have a minimum alcohol content of between 19 and 22%. France imports most of Portugal's production (41%) and the Benelux countries represent the second largest market, buying 21% of all exports.

A port wine cellar.

Lisbon

The capital of Portugal, Lisbon is also the country's main port and largest city. It was founded in 1200 BC by the Phoenicians and conquered successively by various different forces. In 711 four centuries of Arab rule began, during which the city blossomed. Traces of the Moorish city walls remain today. During the Age of Discovery (see below), Lisbon became one of the wealthiest cities in the western world. Much of Lisbon was destroyed in a devastating earthquake in 1755. Many of the city's churches, decorated in baroque, rococo, or rocaille styles, were restored after it, and other parts of the city were also rebuilt. Today Lisbon is a metropolitan city. The Baixa situated at the heart of the city, is the commercial centre. At the port area is the famous tower of Belém. Another notable attraction is the Avenida da Liberdade with its wide blue-mosaic pathways lined with shady palm trees, ornamental fountains and trendy cafes.

The modern Amoreiras Mall in Lisbon.

Fotostock

Explorers

The 15th century was a time of territorial expansion for Portugal. Its geographical location and maritime tradition combined with a desire to reconfirm independence and improve the deteriorating economic situation led to Portugal becoming a forerunner in the Age of Discovery. Prince Henry the Navigator established his school of navigation on the Algarve near Cape Saint Vincent. It was from here that many of the famous Portuguese explorers set off. When Gil Eanes reached Cape Bojador in 1437 after travelling along the coast of Africa, he destroyed the myth of the 'sea of darkness'. Bartolomeu Dias opened the passage to India in 1488, when he went round the aptly named Cape of Good Hope. In 1498 Vasco da Gama reached Calicut and hence realized a dream which had existed in Europe for centuries. Much of the exploration in the Indian Ocean was made possible by the Portuguese invention of the caravel — a vessel capable of negotiating the high seas. In 1519 Magellan, also Portuguese, but in the service of the King of Spain, completed the first circumnavigation of the world.

The explorer, Vasco da Gama.

The Cock of Barcelos

The Portuguese tourist office used the black and red cockerel with the brightly coloured breast as their marketing symbol. This explains why people associate him with Portugal and why every year thousands of tourists buy the pottery cockerel of Barcelos. Barcelos is home to Portugal's largest and most famous pottery market. The story behind it can be traced back to the 14th century. A Galician pilgrim was sentenced to death by hanging. On his way to the gallows he made a roasted cock crow on the judge's dinner table. The pilgrim was set free and the cockerel became a legend.

Fotostock

Algarve

The Algarve is a popular tourist destination for holidaymakers from all the Member States and most people associate it with beaches, night-clubs, and golf. There is, however, another side. The name itself originates from *Al-Gharb*, the Moorish word for 'the West'. Arabic influence is very strong in the architecture and many words commonly used in the Algarve have an Arabic root. Another lesser known fact about the Algarve is that in the month of February it is covered in white. Legend has it that a Moorish king ordered thousands of almond trees to be planted for a northern princess he was in love with. She was pining for the snow-covered hills of her own country and one February morning he took her to the window to show her the snow-white carpet covering the land — the beautiful almond blossoms. They lived happily ever after.

A beach near Portimão, on the Algarve.

Finland has a high reputation for its glassware design.
EKA

Teenager Janne Ahonen is one Finnish ski-jumper who has won gold medals from international championships, and has introduced a new 'V formation' technique to the sport.
Isopress

FINLAND

POPULATION
5 million

CAPITAL
Helsinki

★

1995

Two thirds of the land area is covered by forest, 10% by lakes. The Finnish lake district, a legacy of the last ice age, consists of more than 55 000 lakes which are connected through a series of rivulets. Finland also includes some 179 584 islands. Finnish Lapland lies north of the Arctic Circle. The highest mountain is the Haltiatunturi at 1 324 m and the longest river is the Kemijoki — 494 km.

LAND

The Republic of Finland, (in Finnish, Suomi) lies in northern Europe, bordered to the north by Norway and to the north-west by Sweden. The eastern frontier is bounded by Russia and the Baltic Sea lies to the west and the south. Finland covers an area of more than 338 000 km^2 which is in fact gradually increasing because of the steady uplift of land since the last glacial era.

PEOPLE

Finland has a population of 5 098 427 and an average population density of 16 people per km^2. Approximately 60% of the population live in urban areas. Helsinki has a population of 500 000. The Finns' love of rural life is, however, still evident — there are almost 400 000 summer houses throughout the Finnish countryside.

The largest number of foreign immigrants come from other European countries. In the 1960s there was large-scale emigration from rural Finland to Sweden. A small Lapp population (Sami) live in the north. They have their own language and have to a certain extent retained their traditional lifestyle. There are two official languages in Finland: 93.4% of the population speak Finnish and 5.9% speak Swedish.

ECONOMY

Finland's economy is based on private ownership. Forestry and forestry-related industries such as the pulp and paper industries form the basis of Finland's economy. The biggest growth in recent years has been within the metal industry. This in itself owes a great deal to the forestry industry, as much of the expansion comes from the increased need for machinery and equipment for tree felling and paper production. Other important sectors are telecommunications and high-tech industries, which form a high percentage of exports.

CONSTITUTION AND GOVERNMENT

Finland is a democratic republic. The unicameral parliament (Eduskunta) has 200 members, elected on the basis of proportional representation for four years. The president is the head of State and is elected for a six-year term by direct popular vote. He is responsible for foreign policy and has the power to dissolve the government and call new elections. Legislative power is exercised by parliament. The president appoints the prime minister who, subject to approval, selects the members of the cabinet. They in turn are responsible to parliament. Finland has 12 provinces, each administered by an appointed governor, and is divided into 461 municipalities. The province of Ahvenanmaa (the Aland Islands) has rights of legislation in internal affairs.

The Senate Square, Helsinki.
Markku Ulander

Summers in Finland are often surprisingly warm.
Lehtikuva Oy IS/PN

'What are the first five things that spring to mind when you think about Finland ?'

▶ Lapland - Santa Claus - Forests - Saunas - Telecommunications

Lapland

A region of northern Europe largely within the Arctic Circle, Lapland stretches across northern Norway, Sweden and Finland and into the extreme north-western part of Russia. While Swedish Lapland includes some of the highest peaks in the country, Finnish Lapland is relatively low-lying but still contains Finland's highest mountains. The Sami people are Lapland's original inhabitants, and may have lived in the region for over 7 000 years. A large percentage of the Sami people are bilingual, and the Sami language has almost gained official status in Lapland. They have always had a close relationship with nature, and originally they obtained their livelihood from hunting and fishing. Later, rearing reindeer became increasingly important, particularly for the nomadic part of the Sami people. Today, this nomadic existence is a thing of the past.

Burning bonfires during the midsummer festivities dates from pre-Christian times.

Santa Claus

Santa Claus is a legendary old man who brings gifts to children at Christmas. He lives in Lapland. Originally the idea developed from stories about St Nicholas, a fourth century bishop about whom historians know very little. During the Reformation, protestants substituted non-religious characters for St Nicholas, for example, Father Christmas, Papa Noël and the Weihnachtsmann. Until the 1800s, St Nicholas was pictured as a tall thin stately man who wore bishop's robes and rode a white horse. Finland has over the past few years tried to give Santa Claus a higher commercial profile and a more international image. In 1994, no less than 74 charter flights flew from Heathrow to Finnish Lapland's main city, Rovaniemi, which is close to where Santa Claus and his reindeer live. In fact he receives approximately half a million visitors per year from many different countries.

Matti Björkman

Kimmo Mäntylä

Forests

The addition of Finland to the EU increased the Union's forested area by 35% and paper production by 20%. The forests are considered Finland's national treasure and every effort is made to combine commercial interests with protecting the environment. More than 65% of the forested area is divided into over 400 000 individual holdings. Commonly called the family forestry sector, private ownership is particularly strong in the southern half of the country where the forests enjoy the best conditions for growth. Silviculture and forest exploitation on a small scale are practised here. Most of the State-owned forests are in the region where most of the nature conservation areas are.

Modern technology is helping the forestry industry in Finland.

Saunas

Saunas are justifiably most closely associated with the Finns. Traditionally, wooden enclosures were built near the edge of lakes and rivers. They contained shelf-like rows of flat stones heated by wood fires underneath. When the stones were hot, cold water was thrown on them to create steam. While in the steam hut, bathers beat themselves with branches or paddles until their skin was red and tingling. They then dived into the cold water, or in winter, into the snow. These extreme changes of body temperature were believed to be good for circulation. Today a modern form of the sauna, based on the old principles is still just as popular, and the idea has been exported all over the world.

Skateboarding is widely enjoyed.

Unto Säilä

Telecommunications

In 1887, a year after the telephone was invented, the first telephone line in Finland was already in operation. Telecommunications in Finland have not looked back since, perhaps in part due to the country's harsh climate, long distances and sparse population. The industry is at the forefront of innovation and its characteristically large number of operators (services are currently on offer from 70 telecommunications operators) give it a high international profile as the market is almost fully liberalized and competition highly encouraged. In the 'World competitiveness report 1994', which surveyed the world's most industrialized countries, Finland received the highest marks for systematic IT (information technology) education and in the exploitation of IT products and services. Some 99% of civil servants work in offices with access to electronic mail, and 75% of them use e-mail frequently. Finland's performance is also very impressive with regard to the Internet. In 1995, for example, there were over 97 000 logins from Finland to the European Union's Internet server 'Europa'. Indeed, Finns logged on five times more than the EU average.

*The central area of
Sweden goes from
Stockholm to Göteborg.
Stockholm is both the
political and economic
capital. Göteborg lies on
the west side of the
peninsula and is
Sweden's largest port.
Sweden is bordered
by Finland to the north-
east and by Norway to
the north-west and west.*

SWEDEN

The port of Göteborg,
on Sweden's western coast.
Isopress

LAND

Situated in the centre of northern Europe,
Sweden is the largest (450 000 km²) and most
populated of the nordic States. Half of its land
surface is covered in forest and less than 10% is
farmland. Almost 1 000 lakes dot the
countryside, which is relatively flat. There is a
long mountain chain in the north-west called the
Skanderna. The highest reach heights of up to
2 111 m. There are thousands of islands along
the jagged coast.

PEOPLE

Sweden has a population of 8.8 million, 85% of
which live in the southern half of the country.
The average population density is 21 people per
km². Between 1865 and 1930, there was large-
scale emigration when 1.4 million people left the
country. The main destination was the USA.
During the second half of this century, the tide
turned with more than half a million immigrants ·
moving to Sweden to work. Immigration
accounts for 40% of the population growth and
today over one million of the population are
immigrants or have at least one immigrant
parent. Most come from the other nordic
countries but there are also many from the
former Yugoslavia, Italy, Greece and Turkey.
Political refugees in need of protection account
for a large proportion of the most recent
immigrants.

The national language is Swedish, but there are
Finnish and Lapp (Sami) minorities who have
their own languages. The Sami number between
15 000 and 17 000.

ECONOMY

In the past 100 years Sweden has evolved from a
largely agrarian country to one where less than
3% of the labour force is employed in
agriculture. Manufacturing plays a dominant role
in exports, accounting for more than 80% of
total merchandise and service exports in 1993.
Sweden is renowned as the birthplace of many
well-known multinational corporations which
have helped it to become an affluent country.
Some people would view it as paradoxical that
Sweden also has the world's strongest trade
union movement and a larger public sector than
almost any other western country.

CONSTITUTION AND GOVERNMENT

Sweden is a constitutional monarchy. Today the
monarch has only ceremonial functions as head
of State. Executive power rests with the cabinet
(Regeringen), which is responsible to parliament
(Riksdagen). The unicameral Riksdag was
introduced in January 1971. It has 349 members,
elected by universal adult suffrage for four years
on the basis of proportional representation. The
prime minister is nominated by the speaker of
the Riksdag and later confirmed in office by the
whole House.

The country is divided into 24 counties and 286
municipal districts: both counties and
municipalities have popularly elected councils.
The voting age in Sweden is 18 and voter
turnout is traditionally very high, 85 to 90%.

Sweden's capital, Stockholm.
SIT Stockholm

An example of Sweden's acute
awareness of environmental
issues is shown here with
the manufacture of air filters.
Thomas Nilsson AB

The rap artist Dr Alban was
born in Nigeria, and now
lives in Sweden.
Isopress

'What are the first five things that spring to mind when you think about Sweden ?'

▶ Blondes - Cold - Ingmar Bergman - Nobel prize - Pippi Longstocking

Cold

Sweden is located so far north that the Arctic Circle slices through its northernmost province. It does not, however, have an arctic climate because of the warm Gulf Stream in the Atlantic. Stockholm the capital, is at almost the same latitude as southern Greenland but has an average temperature of about +18°C in July. In the southern part of the country where the majority of the population live, winter temperatures average slightly below freezing and snowfall is moderate. Even white Christmases are a rarity. The far north of Sweden on the other hand has long cold winters and during a certain period there is no daylight at all. However, the summers in the north are bright and enjoy moderate temperatures; in June and July daylight lasts around the clock.

Blondes

The image of Sweden as a nation of blondes has various sources: from the fact that the Vikings were all supposed to be blonde warriors, to the images of the Norse gods and then the Swedish films of the 1950s and 1960s which depicted Swedish women as blondes. In fact, although there are more blondes in Scandinavia than in the Mediterranean countries, Sweden is certainly not the ethnically homogenous country it was in the last century. As stated above, over one million of the population are immigrants.

The pop-group Roxette.

Jonas Linell

n Parys Media

Ingmar Bergman

Bergman is universally recognized as one of the world's most important film-makers. Born in Uppsala, Sweden on 14 July 1918, he attended Stockholm University where he studied art, history, and literature. Whilst there, he also became passionately involved in the theatre and began writing, acting in and directing student productions. Bergman wrote and directed his first film, *Kris* (Crisis) in 1945. This marked the beginning of his film career. In 1955 he had his first international success with *Sommarnattens leende* (*Smiles of a summer night*). This was followed by *The seventh seal* and *Wild strawberries*, both considered masterpieces. Because of the international popularity of Bergman's films, his personal view of Sweden and the Swedish personality were often the first impression the outside world received of Sweden. His image of the country can also be found in the works of other Swedish film-makers, but more because they were so influenced by his work rather than it being the objectively realistic picture.

Ingmar Bergman.

Nobel prize

Alfred Nobel, a 19th-century industrialist, has given his name to the most prestigious academic prizes in the world. He was the inventor of dynamite (patented in 1867) and by exploiting his own and others' inventions he soon became an extremely wealthy man. In his will, Nobel stipulated that the income from his estate should be divided annually into five equal parts and be distributed 'in the form of prizes to those who, during the previous year, have conferred the greatest benefit on mankind.' On 10 December every year since 1901, the King of Sweden has presented the Nobel prizes for literature and the sciences at a ceremony usually held at the Stockholm Concert Hall. The prizes are very prestigious and sometimes leading universities are rated by the number of Nobel prizewinners among their professors and alumni. The literature prize is awarded by the Swedish Academy and the science prizes (physics, chemistry and medicine) by Swedish scientific institutions. The peace prize is awarded in Oslo by a committee of the Norwegian Parliament (Norway was part of a union with Sweden until 1905).

Rabén & Sjögren

Pippi Longstocking

An especially well-known and loved Swede is Pippi Longstocking, the strongest girl on earth. Her creator is the children's author Astrid Lindgren who was born in Vimmerby, Sweden on 14 November 1907. The first of three books with Pippi as its main character appeared in 1945. Since then, her stories have been translated into some 60 languages. Other famous characters include 'Karlson on the roof' and the 'Bullerby children'. Lindgren received the gold medal of the Swedish Academy in 1971. She is also known in Sweden for the use of her sharp pen to comment on political issues.

The children's writer, Astrid Lindgren.

Traditional Scottish Highland dancing.
Isopress

UNITED KINGDOM

POPULATION
58 million

CAPITAL
London

★

1973

The land area is evenly divided between uplands and lowlands. The highest peak is Ben Nevis (1 343 m) situated in the northern Highlands of Scotland. The main rivers are the Thames and the Severn.

LAND

The United Kingdom of Great Britain and Northern Ireland has an area of 244 111 km². It comprises the island of Great Britain — consisting of England which occupies the southern two-thirds of the island, Scotland which occupies the northern third, as well as Wales in the west, and Northern Ireland which lies in the north-eastern part of the island of Ireland. The United Kingdom is separated from the coast of western Europe by the English Channel to the south and by the North Sea to the east. To the north and west lies the Atlantic Ocean.

PEOPLE

The population of the United Kingdom is almost 58 million, with an average population density of 239 inhabitants per km². London has a population of almost seven million. Besides the English (80%), the Scots (9%), the Welsh (5%) and the Northern Irish (3%), the UK population includes 2.5 million foreign residents (1991) — 782 000 of these come from other countries within the Union, two thirds of them from Ireland. The population census in 1991 included for the first time a question on ethnic grouping — 5.5 million described themselves as belonging to a 'non-white' group. Groups included black, Indian, Pakistani, Bangladeshi and Chinese.

ECONOMY

The economy is primarily based on private enterprise, and government policy is aimed at encouraging and expanding the private sector which accounts for approximately 80% of output and 75% of employment. Older industries such as coal, iron, steel, textiles and shipbuilding are currently being reorganized to take account of the shifting patterns in world trade. The 1980s saw the development of high-technology industries and services. These new industries include satellite communications, robotics and information processing.

CONSTITUTION AND GOVERNMENT

The United Kingdom is a constitutional monarchy. The sovereign is the head of State and the monarchy is hereditary. The two Houses of Parliament are the House of Commons and the House of Lords. The 651 members of the Commons are elected for a period of five years by direct suffrage, using single-member constituencies. The House of Lords includes hereditary peers of the realm and life peers and peeresses created by the sovereign for outstanding public service. Legislation may be initiated in either House but it usually originates in the Commons. After three readings of a bill in the Commons, it is then passed to the House of Lords who may return it to the Commons with any amendments or suggestions. The House of Lords may not prevent any bill from becoming law if passed twice by the Commons. They may however delay it. Executive power is held by the Cabinet which is headed by the prime minister. Both he and the Cabinet are responsible to the House of Commons.

Administratively, the United Kingdom is a unitary State in which the parliament is supreme. But both Scotland, which possesses its distinct legal and educational system, and Wales have considerable administrative autonomy which has been delegated by parliament. There is a secretary of State, a Cabinet member for each country and an established regional bureaucracy in both Edinburgh and Cardiff. In 1921 a regional parliament was set up in Belfast (Stormont) to govern the six counties of Northern Ireland. But Stormont was suspended in 1972 and the province is now ruled directly by the Secretary of State for Northern Ireland, a Cabinet member responsible to parliament. Following the local government reforms of 1974, England was divided into 46 counties; Wales has eight counties, and Scotland 12 regions. There are 26 districts in Northern Ireland.

Cambridge has been a seat of learning since the Middle Ages, but sports are important too.
Uwe Wissenbach

Snowdon, the highest peak in the Welsh Cambrian Mountains, reaches a height of 1 085 metres.
Uwe Wissenbach

'What are the first five things that spring to mind when you think about the United Kingdom ?'

▶ Shakespeare - London - BBC - Beatles - The Royals

EKA

Shakespeare

Considered by some to be the greatest dramatist of all time, Shakespeare's plays are performed more often and in more countries than those of any other playwright. Many of his plays have also been taken to the silver screen with such notable actors as Laurence Olivier, Kenneth Brannagh, Emma Thompson and Mel Gibson playing leading roles. It is not known exactly when or in which order Shakespeare's plays were first written. His earliest ones however date from the 1590s, and include *Richard III*, *Henry IV* and *Romeo and Juliet*. Shakespeare also wrote 154 sonnets which are dedicated to someone never named in his writings.

London

London is the capital of the United Kingdom and centre of the Commonwealth. It is situated on both sides of the river Thames in south-eastern England, 64 km from its estuary on the North Sea. Remaining the United Kingdom's largest port, it is also a major centre for international trade and finance. The Tower of London and Tower Bridge have long been symbols of the city. The Tower dates back to the 11th century and has played a significant role in the country's history. The City of Westminster, stretching along the Thames, includes Westminster Abbey and Cathedral, Buckingham Palace, New Scotland Yard and the National Gallery. It is also home to some of the most important shopping districts. Despite the population density in inner London, there are many beautiful and spacious parks, including the oldest of the central royal parks, St James's Park. London has an international population and every nationality seems to have their culinary tastes represented in London's restaurants. London also enjoys a high reputation for its nightlife, and taking in a West End show or going clubbing in one of the more renowned nightclubs is often an essential part of a tourist's trip to the city.

The Channel Tunnel train Eurostar, at London's recently renovated Waterloo station.

Van Parys Medi

BBC

The British Broadcasting Company began as a private corporation in 1922. It became a public corporation, ultimately answerable to Parliament in 1925, and operated a monopoly until 1954. Today the BBC has five radio networks and two television stations. Both media enjoy substantial regional activity. 'National' regions include Scotland, Wales, and Northern Ireland. These regional networks operate by substituting their own programmes for programmes on either Radio 4 or BBC 1. The BBC is also responsible for the United Kingdom's external services and this is one of the reasons why the BBC continues to be recognized abroad. The worldwide service provides transmissions to Europe (from Berlin and Munich), western Asia and the eastern Mediterranean. Of the weekly service, totalling approximately 740 hours, more than one third is in English and the remainder is in almost 40 foreign languages. The principal ones are Arabic, French for Europe and Africa, Russian, German and Spanish for South America. The external services are paid for by annual aid grants from the Treasury.

The BBC's news coverage has an outstanding reputation.
This programme on BBC World, is aimed at the international audience.

Beatles

The Beatles became the most popular rock group in music history. They consisted of four Liverpudlians: George Harrison, John Lennon, Paul McCartney and Ringo Starr. In 1980, Lennon was assassinated outside his New York apartment. While Lennon and McCartney composed most of the songs, Harrison and Starr wrote occasionally. Starr played the drums and the others played the guitar. All of them sang. Their style changed between the early and late 1960s. By the time the Beatles broke up in 1970, their records had outsold those of any other music performers in history. Recently British pop music has undergone something of a renaissance, with groups such as Pulp, Supergrass, Elastica, Blur and particularly Oasis (together dubbed 'Brit-pop') writing and performing their own blend of self-conscious lyrics and up-beat guitar-based tunes. Inheriting a style that owes much to the Beatles, the Manchester-based band Oasis have taken the music scene by storm since the release of their first single *Supersonic*, in the spring of 1994. Their recent album, *(What's the story) Morning glory?* has gone quadruple platinum, and remains a bestseller throughout Europe.

Oasis, *Wonderwall*.

The Royals

The British royal family consists of Queen Elizabeth II and her nearest relatives. The monarchy is the oldest institution of government, dating back to the ninth century, at least. The Queen represents the State and is regarded as a symbol of national unity. She is head of the Commonwealth, the law, the armed forces and the Church of England. Members of her family share in her work by representing her in ceremonies and visits.

The city of Glasgow in west Scotland is a superb example of one of the UK's northern cities that is enjoying regeneration and renewed dynamism.

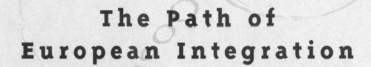

The Path of
European Integration

N. Paschalidis

The Acropolis in Athens is symbolic of the European origins of democracy and also a witness to the passing centuries which have seen its architecture emulated in many forms.

Eureka Slide

The durability of Europe's shared cultures and values is exemplified in this painting of a family from Pompei.

Shared values

As this booklet so vividly demonstrates, Europe encompasses a kaleidoscope of languages, cultures, traditions and landscapes. Its diversity is a testament to the innovation and creativity of its inhabitants, peoples who despite maintaining their differences, have many values in common.

▶

Erasmus.
Eureka Slide

The origins of the European Union

The democratic form of government bequeathed to us by the Greeks was to become a cornerstone of European civilization. With their written law, the Romans endowed Europe with the rules which order our relations with each other. In the 16th and 17th centuries, the likes of Copernicus, Galileo, Kepler, Descartes, Huygens and Newton paved the way for modern science.

Before the advent of nationalism, 'European careers' were quite normal. Craftsmen plied their trade all over the continent, learning as they went from one country to the next, without worrying about borders. Erasmus, who was born in Rotterdam 500 years ago, studied in Paris, obtained a doctorate in Turin and taught in Cambridge for more than a decade. He died in Basle. Despite the many languages and regional dialects, the knowledge of philosophers and scientists spread everywhere, contributing to the cross-fertilization of ideas. Artists from all countries met to exchange ideas. The peoples of Europe have always been linked by a shared culture.

POPULATION BY AGE GROUP

on 1 January 1993

	0-14	15-24	25-44	45-64	65+	Total
B	1 829.4	1 330.8	3 067.6	2 290.5	1 550.0	→ 10 068.3
DK	882.6	722.2	1 550.4	1 222.0	803.3	→ 5 180.6
D	13 241.9	9 970.0	25 333.8	20 252.8	12 176.2	→ 80 974.6
GR	1871.5	1 557.5	2 877.9	2 530.0	1 512.3	→ 10 349.2
E	7 021.7	6 494.7	11 386.1	8 578.8	5 566.7	→ 39 048.0
F	11 458.4	8 279.0	17 284.3	12 147.2	8 360.8	→ 57 529.7
IRL	920.9	610.2	971.2	650.1	407.5	→ 3 560.0
I	8 830.5	8 635.9	16 666.2	13 877.4	8 950.3	→ 59 960.3
L	70.8	48.8	129.8	92.0	53.9	→ 395.2
NL	2 791.1	2 202.2	4 922.3	3 338.1	1 985.6	→ 15 239.3
AT	1 399.1	1 120.5	2 487.3	1 769.6	1 185.4	→ 7 962.0
P	1 860.1	1 637.7	2 760.5	2 222.4	1 384.0	→ 9 864.6
FI	968.3	636.5	1 579.7	1 175.2	695.3	→ 5 055.0
SE	1 606.0	1 117.9	2 430.9	2 002.7	1534.5	→ 8 692.0
UK	11 252.6	7 845.7	17 049.3	12 795.5	9 155.8	→58 098.9
EUR 15	66 004.8	52 209.6	110 497.3	84 944.2	55 321.7	→368 977.7

Aggression resulting from the economic and technological power created by 19th and 20th century industrialization and nationalism broke up this cultural symbiosis. In the aftermath of the Second World War, Jean Monnet and Robert Schuman persuaded six former wartime enemies (Belgium, France, Germany, Italy, Luxembourg and the Netherlands), to come together and discuss how the terrible events of former decades could be prevented from ever happening again. In 1952, the European Coal and Steel Community came into being, tying together the heavy industries of these six nations. As Robert Schuman said, 'If you no longer have full control over energy and steel, you can no longer declare war'. Peace was the guiding principle behind this coalition.

Greater unity was heralded in 1958 when the European Economic Community (EEC) and the European Atomic Energy Community (Euratom) were set up by the Treaties of Rome (1957). Since that time, the Community has grown from its six original members, to include Denmark, Ireland and the United Kingdom in 1973, Greece in 1981, and Spain and Portugal in 1986. The population of the Community increased by 18 million with the reunification of Germany in 1990, and in 1993 what had been the European Community became the European Union. Finally in 1995, Austria, Finland and Sweden joined the Union, bringing together 370 million inhabitants, a land area of 3 337 000 km² and 15 member countries.

EKA

Managing the European Union (EU)

To manage the policies concerning such a large population, the Union has a system of institutions that work in collaboration with each other, undertaking the principles of safeguarding peace and promoting economic and social progress. These institutions are:

The European Council, made up of the Heads of State or Government of the Member States which meets at least twice a year, and traces out guidelines on Union policy;

The Council of the European Union, often referred to as the Council of Ministers, brings together ministers from the 15 Member States who have responsibility for the area to be discussed — foreign affairs, agriculture, industry, transport, the environment — and so on. It enacts European law, and with the European Parliament, has joint control over legislation and the Union's budget;

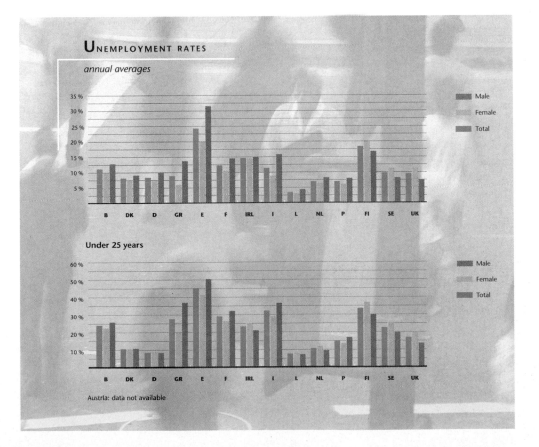

The European Commission consists of 20 members who pledge to serve the Union's interests, not their national governments'. Most of the Commissioners have served earlier as ministers or MPs. They provide it with political leadership and direction. The Commission is the largest EU institution, and it acts as guardian of the Treaties, ensuring that legislation and directives adopted by the Council are implemented. It also initiates the proposals for the laws that are put before the Council and Parliament, and can intervene at any point in the legislative process. Finally, it is often the Commission that suggests ways in which the Union should develop. It is appointed by agreement between member governments after approval by the European Parliament. Parliament (in a capacity that has never been used), can pass a motion of censure, compelling the Commission to resign as a body;

The European Parliament is a democratic forum for debate with the power of co-decision in important areas. It currently has 626 members who are elected every five years (the first elections being held in 1979), and who meet in Strasbourg for a monthly plenary session and in Brussels for committee meetings. It often works in parallel with the Council in a legislative capacity, and since the Treaty on European Union came into force (1993), it has enjoyed greater influence, by having the power of co-decision in certain areas i.e. European law cannot be enacted without Parliament's consent, notably regarding the single market and agreements with other countries;

The European Court of Justice together with the Court of First Instance ensures that EU law is observed. It has 15 judges, assisted by nine advocates-general. The Court of First Instance, set up in 1989 also has 15 judges. Actions may be brought by Member States, EU institutions and by individual citizens and companies;

The Economic and Social Committee is a consultative body consisting of 222 members divided into three groups, employers, workers and other interests (farmers, craftsmen, small and medium-sized manufacturing and other businesses, the professions, representatives of consumers, the scientific and teaching community, cooperatives, families and ecological movements). It must be consulted by the Council and the Commission before decisions are made on many subjects, and it can also issue opinions on its own initiative;

The Committee of the Regions is also a consultative body, on matters of regional importance notably education, youth, culture, public health, economic and social cohesion, and trans-European transport, telecommunications and energy networks. Set up by the Treaty on European Union, it may issue opinions on regional issues;

The European Investment Bank is the Union's financing institution and provides long-term loans for capital investment promoting the Union's balanced economic development and integration; and finally, **The Court of Auditors** audits EU budget operations.

One of the main subjects under discussion at the Intergovernmental Conference (a series of meetings between the ministers of Member States) that began in March 1996 in Turin is how the institutions must grow and evolve to take into account changes likely due to further enlargement of the European Union. All the institutions also follow the principle of 'openness', attempting to be more open to the public they serve. 'Subsidiarity' is another guiding principle, which means that the Union only addresses issues that are best served on a European level, and will leave other matters for individual national governments. Thus education mostly remains in the national domain, and the environment is increasingly a Union matter.

The single market and monetary union

A single market is of great importance to all the citizens of the European Union. There have been no customs duties within the Community since 1968, and common rates of duty have been applied to imports from non-member countries. On 1 January 1993 the plan for a single European market came to fruition. Border checks were removed. Only in rare cases are random checks still carried out. It is now easier for firms to offer their goods and services in other EU countries. The free movement of capital makes it possible to invest money anywhere in the Union. Perhaps the most important innovation is the free movement of persons: Union citizens are entitled to travel, reside, study and work wherever they wish in the European Union.

Anyone is entitled to apply for a job and sign a contract of employment in another Member State: no one may be discriminated against on grounds of nationality. Pension and health insurance entitlements acquired in another Member State are not lost. Union citizens can carry on the occupation in which they have been trained thanks to the mutual recognition of qualifications. The EU helps its citizens to gain experience abroad by means of exchange schemes, such as the educational programme 'Socrates'.

Do you think that, to make further progress in building Europe, it is necessary or not to have **a single internal market?**

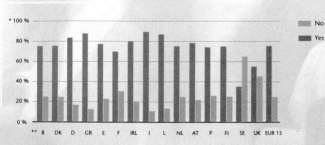

No
Yes

* 100 %
80 %
60 %
40 %
20 %
0 %

** B DK D GR E F IRL I L NL AT P FI SE UK EUR 15

▶ As these figures indicate, the vast majority of Europeans feel that it is necessary to have a single internal market. Only in Sweden, did a majority not feel this to be a necessity.

* Percentage not shown: don't know.

** Countries B - Belgium, DK - Denmark, D - Germany, GR - Greece, E - Spain, F - France, IRL - Ireland, I - Italy, L - Luxembourg, NL - The Netherlands, AT - Austria, P - Portugal, FI - Finland, SE - Sweden, UK - The United Kingdom, and EUR 15 - an average of all 15 countries of the European Union.

Figures taken from 'Eurobarometer 44.2 bis - Mega-survey', March 1996.

EKA

Travel and shopping has also become easier for Union citizens. They can buy goods for personal use anywhere in the EU and take them back home with them without having to pay any more taxes. (There are exceptional rules for new cars.)

Coupled with the idea of the single market is economic and monetary union. This will manifest itself most visibly for EU citizens with the advent of a European currency, the 'euro' at the turn of the century, backed by an independent European central bank. A European currency will make it even easier to travel, live, trade and work in another Member State. Other benefits will be no foreign exchange commissions, an end to speculative dealing, increased price transparency aiding competition and the consumer, and a strong international currency. All this will result in renewed growth and competitiveness for business in Europe and thus also foster job creation.

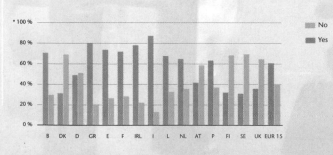

Do you think that, to make further progress in building Europe, it is necessary to have **one European currency?**

No
Yes

► Support for a single currency varies significantly from country to country.
It is interesting to note, however, that three quarters of European Union citizens interviewed found the name for the currency, 'euro' acceptable.

* Percentage not shown: don't know.

Figures taken from 'Eurobarometer 44.2 bis — Mega-survey', March 1996.

Much research is underway in Europe to improve the quality of life. The photo shows solar cells being manufactured for sunlight collectors to produce clean energy.

Other key policy areas of the EU

Regional policy

The Union's aim of promoting social progress is illustrated through its commitment to reducing the disparities between the different regions of the Union. In the most affluent regions, earnings are four times as high as in the poorest. The goal of reducing these great disparities was accordingly written into the founding Treaties themselves. It is primarily the Structural Funds which are used to ensure that the inhabitants of the disadvantaged regions have a decent standard of living. In 1996, 33.7% of the Union's total financial expenditure is set aside for regional and social projects, and this percentage is increasing yearly.

Agriculture

The common agricultural policy (CAP) is perhaps the most well-known Union policy. It underwent radical reform in 1992, after becoming a victim of its own success, by penalizing overproduction and bringing agricultural activities in fields such as conservation of the countryside and environmental protection into the foreground. Extensive farming and ecological agriculture — involving a quantitatively lower but qualitatively higher level of production — are promoted particularly strongly.

The environment

Protection of the environment is perhaps one area of Union policy where the need for common policies is most apparent. Pollution is no respecter of national boundaries. The Union's position is a proactive rather than a reactive one. In other words, programmes are now in place to prevent environmental degradation, rather than correct it. The emphasis is on sustainability. For example, the EU has undertaken to ban the production and consumption of CFCs (chlorofluorocarbons that contribute to the depletion of the ozone layer that protects the earth from ultraviolet radiation which is a possible cause of skin disease) by 1997. Today, the production of CFCs is only 45% of what it was in 1988, and the production of CFCs from propellants (the most serious type of pollutant) has fallen to 10% of its 1987 figure.

Van Parys Media

▶ Virtual reality, developed as a leisure activity, also has more practical applications allowing information to be gathered and analysed where it would be difficult or impossible for a human to go, such as geological research in the sea bed.

Young people

Europe's future lies with its young people, and the EU undertakes various educational and training programmes to help ensure that the young realize their potential. 'Socrates' is a programme launched to promote higher education exchanges, and the learning of languages. Another programme, 'Leonardo' has the primary aim of aiding people to obtain technical and industrial training and forging links between industry and education. Finally 'Youth for Europe' encourages cooperation between youth organizations in different countries.

The information society

Multimedia and new technology are changing the workplace and allowing information to be passed across vast areas instantaneously. The advent of the information society has created a rapidly expanding market that the European Union must acknowledge and be a part of if it is to remain competitive. The Union is committed to opening up the telecommunications sector of this market, for example, to encourage competition and innovation. Similarly, new technology is being implemented by the Union through major trans-European networks: projects in the fields of telecommunications, energy and transport.

Some people expect the European Union to become (even) more active than now in certain areas. For each of the following, please tell me if you consider it a key priority or not:

EU policy areas	Making joint efforts to better protect the environment	Ensuring that each member country's academic and professional training qualifications are recognized throughout the EU	Providing more opportunities to find a job anywhere in the European Union	Developing joint programmes to fight against unemployment	Fighting together against cancer, AIDS, etc.
% of 15-24 year old Europeans *					
Key priority	87.2	80.1	85.1	89.1	89.4
Not key priority	12.8	19.9	14.9	10.9	10.6

▶ Young people are obviously concerned about numerous issues regarding the European Union. These figures show that young Europeans have the greatest worries about employment, the environment and medical research, followed by their support for more active policies on such issues as equal opportunities between men and women, protecting consumers, supporting the poorer regions of the European Union, and making the European Union even closer to the citizens.

Figures taken from 'Eurobarometer 44.2 bis — Mega-survey', March 1996.
* Percentage not shown: don't know.

EKA

The European Union is committed
to numerous aid programmes
throughout the world, and is in
fact the world's largest donor.

Eureka Slide

The Union's external relations

The challenge of the future expansion of the Union is increasingly pressing. Early next century, the Union could consist of up to 30 Member States including many of the former communist States of Central and Eastern Europe and two Mediterranean countries — Malta and Cyprus — both of which have accession negotiations already scheduled for the near future. This poses not only a social challenge, but also an economic one. In 1993 the per capita gross domestic product amongst the 10 countries which have Europe Agreements with the EU (Poland, the Czech Republic, Slovakia, Hungary, Bulgaria, Romania, Estonia, Latvia, Lithuania and Slovenia) was only 12% of the EU's figure for GDP per capita. Europe Agreements cover various areas of policy with the aim of bringing the signatory countries closer to the European Union. Democracy, human rights and a market economy are all obligatory conditions to any agreement. The agreements themselves cover several main areas including: political dialogue, economic operations, rules on competition, property, monetary transfers and legislation, and cooperation of a cultural nature. They are a technical preparation for eventual membership to the European Union. To finance the reduction in the disparities between the Union and these countries, the EU has committed large funds to programmes such as PHARE and TACIS. It is in Europe's interest to encourage the expansion of the Union so that it covers as wide an area as possible, for economic, social, environmental and perhaps most importantly, political reasons.

The Union also has cooperation agreements with virtually all the Mediterranean countries covering trade, industrial cooperation, technical and financial assistance.

More broadly, the European Union has a prominent role to play globally. Already the world's leading trade power, it shares practices and aims with other major trading blocks such as the United States of America and Japan, but is also their rival commercially and technologically. As the EU is such a strong economic power, it has a particularly influential bargaining position during talks on trade. The last series of these talks — the Uruguay Round — which involved discussions amongst 117 countries, ended in 1994 with the signing of a broad-reaching treaty on trade. This treaty substantially liberalizes international trade and has created the World Trade Organization (WTO), which is a new and stronger supervisory body. The European Union emerged considerably strengthened from the lengthy negotiations, its pivotal role (along with the United States) allowing it to reach agreements on contentious issues such as subsidized farm exports.

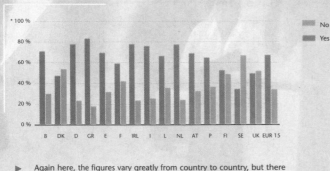

Do you think that, to make further progress in building Europe, it is necessary to have **one European foreign policy?**

No
Yes

* 100 %
80 %
60 %
40 %
20 %
0 %

B   DK   D   GR   E   F   IRL   I   L   NL   AT   P   FI   SE   UK   EUR 15

▶   Again here, the figures vary greatly from country to country, but there is general agreement by a majority of Europeans that a European foreign policy is necessary.

Figures taken from 'Eurobarometer 44.2 bis — Mega-survey', March 1996.
* Percentage not shown: don't know.

However, the Union is not a protectionist bloc. Developing countries see the Union as their main market, because it offers them preferential access for most of their industrial and agricultural products. Indeed, the EU has special arrangements — set up through the fourth Lomé Convention — with 70 countries in Africa, the Caribbean and the Pacific (ACP countries). These countries also enjoy economic and social investment support via the European Development Fund. Cooperation between the European Union and developing countries in Asia and Latin America is not so advanced, but progress is constantly being made.

What lies ahead for the European Union?

Obviously the future expansion of the Union, successfully achieving monetary union, promoting further links with developing countries and obtaining agreement at the Intergovernmental Conference on matters such as human rights, employment, internal security, simplification of the treaties, the EU's role in the world commercially and strategically, and restructuring the institutions, are all areas that will be given close consideration in the near future. However, it should not be forgotten why we need the Union in general terms, and need it to develop. It must progress and evolve not to fulfil some ideology of its creators, but because we live in a constantly changing world, and it must reflect and adapt to these changes. The EU is only what its citizens want it to be, it was created to serve their interests, and that aim remains constant. On the threshold of the 21st century, no one can predict exactly how the European Union will develop — we have no precedent to follow — but the essential ingredient is the active, informed participation of its people.

European Commission

Exploring Europe

Luxembourg: Office for Official Publications of the European Communities

1996 — 78 pp. — 21 x 29.7 cm

ISBN 92-827-7595-X

This booklet describes the principal characteristics of the 15 Member States of the European Union, their geography, political system and economy.

It also outlines the main landmarks, institutions and policies in the process of European integration.

It is primarily intended for young people and schools.

European Commission

Rue de la Loi 200, B-1049 Bruxelles

BELGIQUE/BELGIË

Rue Archimède 73
B-1000 BRUXELLES
Archimedesstraat 73
B-1000 BRUSSEL
Tél. (32-2) 295 38 44
Fax (32-2) 295 01 66

DANMARK

Højbrohus
Østergade 61
Postbox 144
DK-1004 KØBENHAVN K
Tlf. (45) 33 14 41 40
Fax (45) 33 11 12 03/14 13 92 (sekretariat)
     (45) 33 14 14 47 (dokumentation)

DEUTSCHLAND

Zitelmannstraße 22
D-53113 BONN
Postfach 53106 BONN
Tel. (49-228) 53 00 90
Fernkopie (49-228) 53 00 950/12

Kurfürstendamm 102
D-10711 BERLIN
Tel. (49-30) 896 09 30
Fernkopie (49-30) 892 20 59

Erhardtstraße 27
D-80331 MÜNCHEN
Tel. (49-89) 202 10 11
Fernschreiber (041) 52 18 135
Fernkopie (49-89) 202 10 15

GREECE/ΕΛΛΑΔΑ

Vassilissis Sofias 2
T.K. 30 284
GR-106 74 ATHINA
Tel. (30-1) 725 10 00
Telefax (30-1) 724 46 20

ESPAÑA

Paseo de la Castellana, 46
E-28046 MADRID
Tel. (34-1) 431 57 11
Fax (34-1) 576 03 87/577 29 23

Av. Diagonal, 407 bis, 18^a
E-08008 BARCELONA
Tel. (34-3) 415 81 77 (5 líneas)
Fax (34-3) 415 63 11

FRANCE

288, boulevard Saint-Germain
F-75007 PARIS
Pour obtenir les publications:
Centre d'information et de documentation
«Sources d'Europe»
Socle de la Grande Arche
F-92054 Paris La Défense Cedex 61
Tél. (33-1) 41 25 12 12

CMCI
2, rue Henri Barbusse
F-13241 MARSEILLE Cedex 01
Tél. (33) 91 91 46 00
Fax (33) 91 90 98 07

IRELAND

Jean Monnet Centre
18 Dawson Street
DUBLIN 2
Tel. (353-1) 662 51 13
Fax (353-1) 662 51 18

ITALIA

Via Poli, 29
I-00187 ROMA
Tel. (39-6) 699 991
Telecopia (39-6) 679 16 58/679 36 52

Corso Magenta, 59
I-20123 MILANO
Tel. (39-2) 48 01 25 05
Telecopia (39-2) 481 85 43

LUXEMBOURG

Bâtiment Jean Monnet
Rue Alcide De Gasperi
L-2920 LUXEMBOURG
Tél. (352) 43 01-34925
Fax (352) 43 01-34433

NEDERLAND

Korte Vijverberg 5
NL-2513 AB DEN HAAG
Postbus 30465
NL-2500 GL DEN HAAG
Tel. (31-70) 346 93 26
Telefax (31-70) 364 66 19

ÖSTERREICH

Hoyosgasse 5
A-1040 WIEN
Tel. (43-1) 505 33 79
Fax (43-1) 505 33 797

PORTUGAL

Centro Europeu Jean Monnet
Largo Jean Monnet, 1-10.º
P-1200 LISBOA
Tel. (351-1) 350 98 00
Telecópia (351-1) 355 43 97/
   /350 98 01/350 98 02/350 98 03

SUOMI/FINLAND

Pohjoisesplanadi 31
PL 234
FIN-00131 HELSINKI
Norra esplanaden 31
PB 234
FIN-00131 HELSINGFORS
Puh. (358-0) 65 64 20
Fax (358-0) 65 67 28

SVERIGE

Box 7323
Hamngatan 6
S-103 90 STOCKHOLM
Tel. (46-8) 611 11 72
Fax (46-8) 611 44 35

UNITED KINGDOM

Jean Monnet House
8 Storey's Gate
LONDON SW1P 3AT
Tel. (44-71) 973 19 92
Fax (44-71) 973 19 00/19 10/18 95

Windsor House
9/15 Bedford Street
BELFAST BT2 7EG
Tel. (44-232) 24 07 08
Fax (44-232) 24 82 41

4 Cathedral Road
CARDIFF CF1 9SG
Tel. (44-222) 37 16 31
Fax (44-222) 39 54 89

9 Alva Street
EDINBURGH EH2 4PH
Tel. (44-31) 225 20 58
Fax (44-31) 226 41 05

UNITED STATES OF AMERICA

2300 M Street, NW
WASHINGTON, DC 20037
Tel. (202) 862 95 00
Fax (202) 429 17 66

3 Dag Hammarskjöld Plaza
305 East 47th Street
NEW YORK, NY 10017
Tel. (212) 371 38 04
Fax (212) 758 27 18/688 10 13

NIPPON

Europa House
9-15 Sanbancho
Chiyoda-Ku
TOKYO 102
Tel. (813) 239 04 41
Fax (813) 32 39 93 37/32 61 51 94